W9-AUH-311

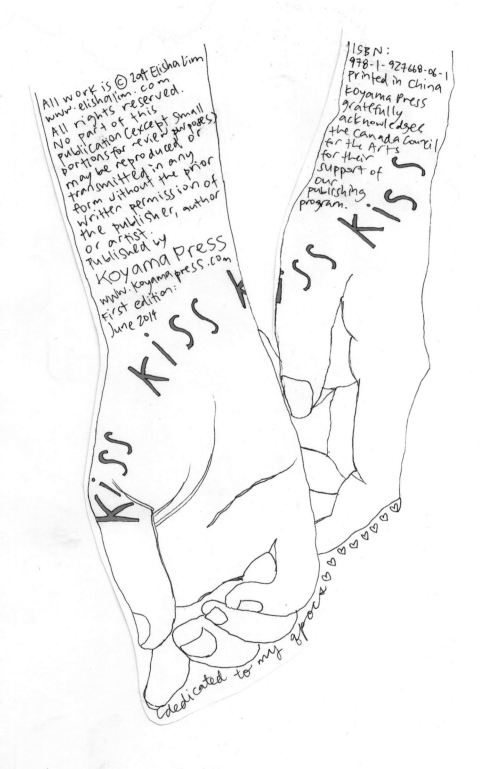

Published by
Koyama Press
www.koyamapress.com
First edition:
June 2014

ISBN:
978-1-927668-06-1
Printed in China
Koyama Press
gratefully
acknowledges
the Canada Council
for the Arts
for their
support of
our
publishing
program.

Kiss Kiss Kiss Kiss Kiss

dedicated to my gforce

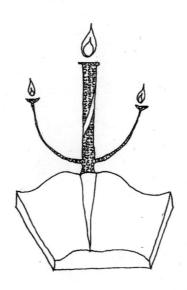

100 Butches has been featured in British, American and Australian lesbian magazines, Michelle Tea's literary tour across America, the legendary Toronto FAG gallery, and claymation shorts that have screened in film festivals worldwide. Which blows my mind, all things considered.

It started while I was sitting on a London bus wishing I was doing anything other than going to my waiter job. I'd read that Diva Magazine was looking for a new lesbian cartoonist, and I thought I'd give it a shot. I pulled out my server's notepad and started sketching.

When I got home I wrote the most ambitious and untrue email. "I'm a lesbian cartoonist," I lied, "and I'm very proud of my strip. It's called One Hundred Butches and it's exactly that: an illustrated catalogue of 100 fabulous butch lesbians that I've encountered."

They took a chance on me, and it changed everything. They ran my comics and even introduced me to my comic hero Alison Bechdel. This is an excerpt of the most magical undertaking of my life.

100 Butches

One Hundred Butches | Number Two

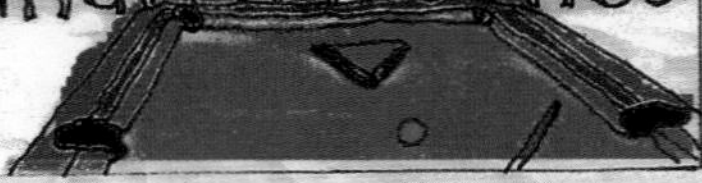

My aunt called herself the black sheep of the family. There was no point denying it, she didn't fit in.

I found her irresistible. Out of all of my thirty aunts, I would hunt for her at reunions. I'd ask, "is she coming today?" Sometimes I was relieved when she wasn't. She would say crude things and laugh uproariously at me, like "hold this, it's my boyfriend's penis." My grief would make her cry with laughter, but it made me love her even more. Her rude sense of humour seemed so pleasingly unpretentious.

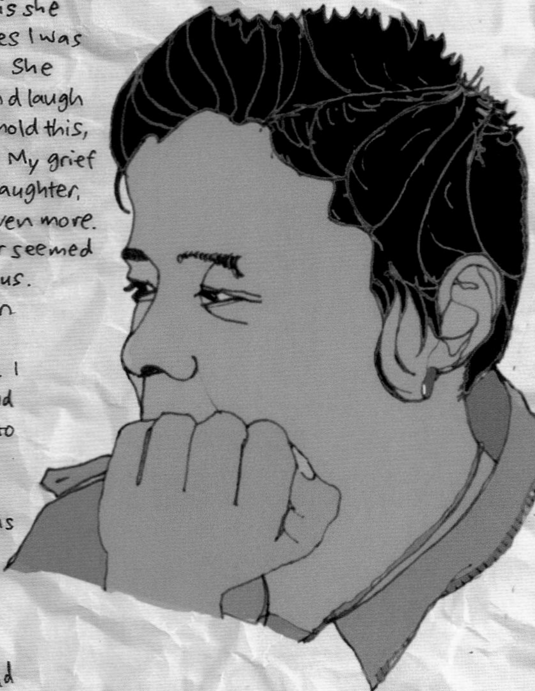

When I visited Malaysia in my twenties, she made every effort to corrupt me. I phoned her up and she and her girlfriend took me out to bars. She would kneel down in front of me and say "slap my hands." It was the kind of drinking game that I didn't find fun, but something about the quality time made it worthwhile. Later she would look seriously into my face, and say, "why don't you come out?" She figured it out long before I did.

The last time I visited Malaysia, homosexuality was still illegal. I went out with her and she sat despondently under the weird light of a pool hall. I realized looking at her that she had become a black sheep in public, too. My friends had taught me the signals of the local gangs, and I felt a bit afraid.

May she forgive me. I owe her my understanding, more than any other sheep in the herd. It's been a long time now, and I can't wait to find her again.

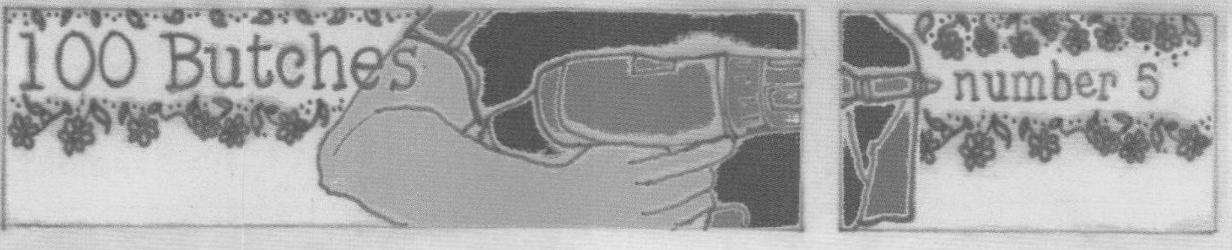
100 Butches
number 5

I was walking home from work one day in a small Spanish town. As I passed a construction site, a crowd of workers came out to take a break. One of them sat quietly and just stared into the distance while the others ate and talked loudly.

She was basically just sitting there. But how do you explain the moment when you just get knocked out by someone? How do you describe that effect, when you just think whoa, baby.

It was only a couple of gestures- she took off her hat with a swing, she ran her hand through her hair, she bent down to light her cigarette. That was it. I skipped a breath and whistled quietly with cat calls shrieking inside my head.

I wanted a line to use the next time I saw her. I even went and looked it up in a dictionary. I found a good one, "estás como un tren," which turned up next to "beautiful."

"Oh no," said my co-worker Ariadne the next day. "You don't want to say that. That means you are hot and I want you, grr, grr." She demonstrated by grinding against a chair. Perfect, I thought. I kept my route home the same every day. But to my disappointment, I never saw her again.

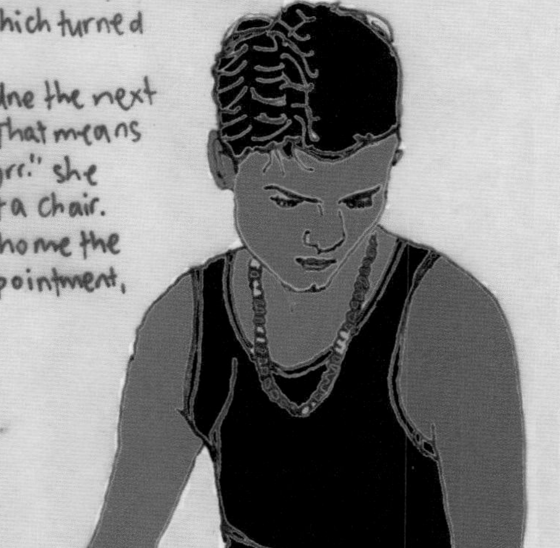

ONE HUND
BUTCHES

NUMBEREIGHT

I thought Ruby was the epitome of sexy. She was a gymnast, a taekwon do expert, a netball center, a javelin thrower and a Singaporean chess master, and we were thirteen. She would unbutton her collar and strut nonchalantly up the class line. "What's up, Fish?" she would tease, and then inflict on me some kind of painful salute. It left me speechless with admiration. She sat next to me during history class and I made a futile year-long attempt to break through the macho smalltalk. At the end of the year we had an exam and she slouched deeper and deeper into her desk until her uniform rode up her legs, and I realized that the answers were scribbled onto her thighs.

I concentrated badly, needless to say. In my diary it says "second period, history exam," and then, "am I gay?"

Since then I've heard that she married the frontman of a rock band.

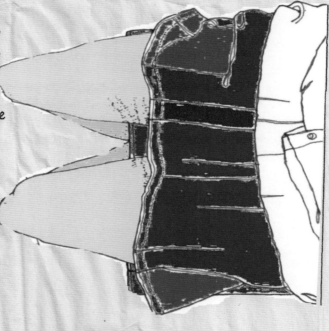

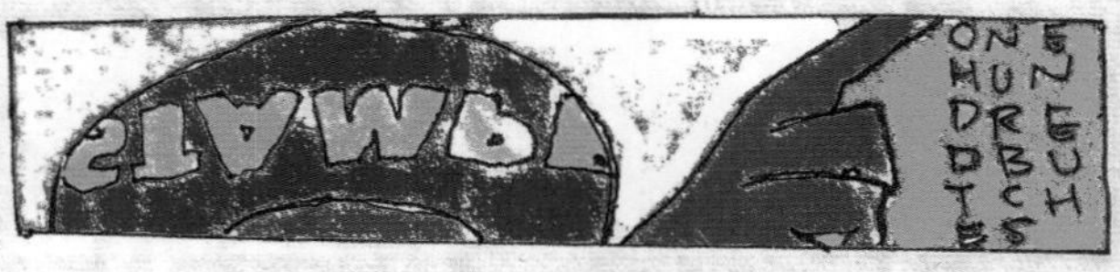
ONE HUNDRED BUTCHES

NUMBER TEN

One night at a party I asked Lunah B how she felt about being called a butch. Our friends had different things to say. "I don't relate to butch," said Leasha, "because it's usually used by and for white people."

I thought about it, and it was hard to argue. Where did I first hear the word? Leslie Feinberg's 'Stone Butch Blues,' Ellen DeGeneres' 'If These Walls Could Talk,' Country Music Television. Toyin agreed.

"Butch makes me think of flannel shirts, mullets and white working class appropriation."

"Wow," I said.

"Yeah wow," she said. "Do you see me dressing like that?" We all shook our heads. She said, "I call myself the names of Black queer families, like a stud or an a.g. But I'm a soft a.g."

"What about you, Lunah B?" I said, "what are you?"

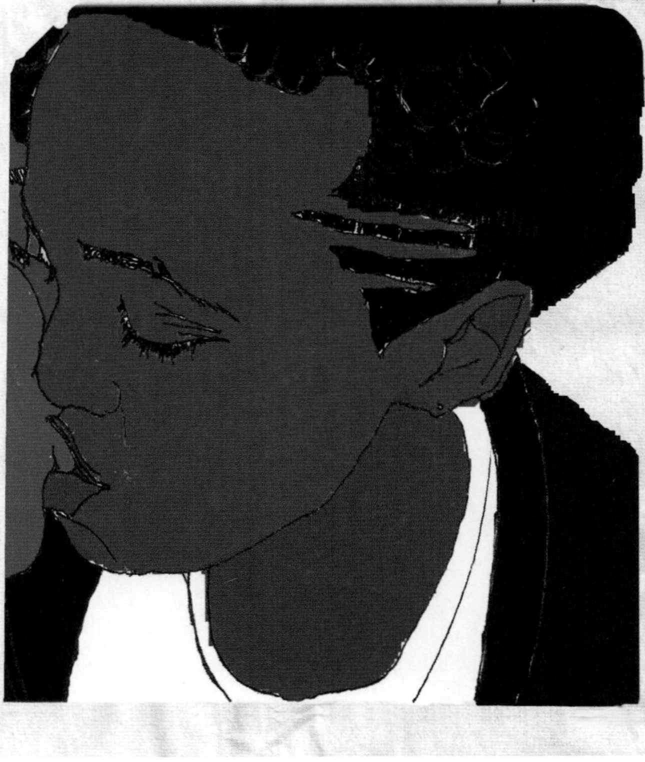

"How about a stemme?" she said. "Like a stud and a femme. I've only heard it used by Black dykes. It's used to describe androgynous people, for more gender fluidity."

It was a lot to think about, and I struggled with it all as the party loosened up around me. I had to grin in appreciation watching Lunah B work her way through the crowd. My first stemme encounter. I decided I liked it.

Back in Singapore I was known as an "active." When I got to the West I became known as a "butch." It wasn't a good shift. I felt like I became impotent somehow. When I walked into the room I didn't get checked out in the same way.

I think that we butches have to think about the social associations of masculinity, and that changes depending on our race. It's not an obvious conclusion, but I think it's true.

I had to stop and ask myself, do people read me as masculine? Do they see my Chinese race first? And what does that do to their perception of masculinity?

I think that Chinese male stereotypes aren't very romantic: harmless, dependable, quiet and effeminate.

As a result, my normal performance of masculinity has now been interrupted by all these extra layers of emasculating preconceptions.

You could call it a classic case of culture shock. When you move there's so much you leave behind. Back at home I was part of a majority. Now I am part of the margins. When I moved to the States, I didn't expect my sex appeal to suffer!

At least, this is my theory. You can disagree with me. But frankly, when I was preparing myself to walk into a party as a butch, with my collar up and my hair all styled, on some unconscious level I was attempting to adopt a different gender but also to adopt a different race. I was trying to pass as the archetypical man: the white man. Nowadays I've decided to create my own show. I dress for myself, and I imitate my own East Asian male role models, like Andy Lau and Bi. I sport fur coats, sunglasses indoors, and bleached tips. Maybe the girls don't get it, but in time they will. Chinese men are sexy! If that's a reference that I can draw on, then I count myself lucky.

100 Butches Number 20

湖俠瑾
鑑女秋

There are some stories that are hard to find. All I can find are clues, like Qiu Jin, and helpful friends like professor Vivien Ng, but they're still worth sharing.

From about 1865 to 1935, a women's sect developed in three districts of southern China called The Golden Orchid Society of Marriage Resisters. They referred to their husbands' families as "cocoons" that bound their bodies and deprived them of freedom. A national propriety census claimed that they engaged in forbidden behaviour: "Although cohabiting women do not possess the form of male-female sexual relationships, they do possess the pleasure of such relationships. Suffice to say that they use friction and, or, mechanical means; to say more requires the use of inelegant language which gentlemen cannot use."

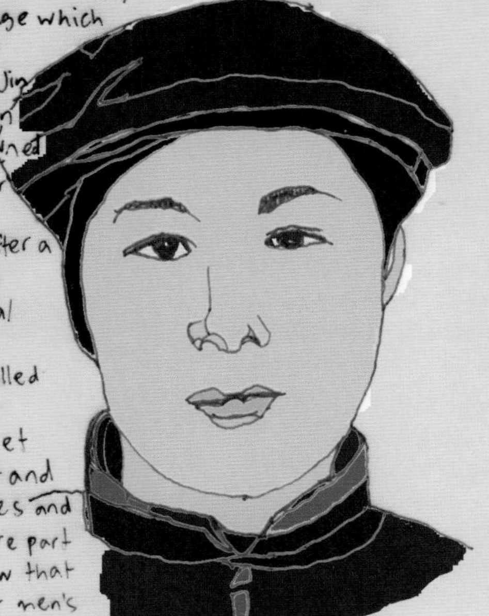

Was national hero Qiu Jin one of these women? In 1903 she met the renowned calligrapher and reformer Wu Zheying, and they became inseparable. After a year they exchanged a "formal pledge of eternal friendship," which they marked with a poem called "Orchid Verse."

The next day Qiu Jin met Zheying in a man's suit and gave her a pair of shoes and skirt, saying, "These were part of my bridal effects. Now that I have decided to wear men's clothes, I have no need for them."

She became a martyr in 1907 when the occupying Qing government executed her for attempting a coup. This dubious honour might make her the most famous symbol of the Golden Orchid Society of Marriage Resisters.

100 Butches

Ma Rainey

Twenty Two

At first I wanted to pay tribute to Ma Rainey because in 1932, she wrote gay anthems. "Folks say I'm crooked," she sang, "I want the whole world to know."

I drew her picture for magazines. I organized tribute concerts. I drew posters based on her photos, with her dangly earrings, sashes and jewels. I thought to myself, what a courageous femme.

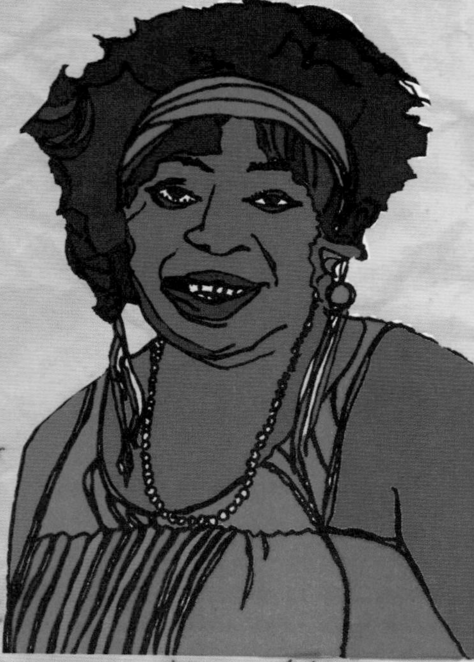

Then one day I was singing her song on my bicycle. "It's true I wear a collar and a tie." I flipped my collar up and jutted my chin. "I talk to the gals like any old man." I tried to growl just like she might have.

It struck me suddenly, with my suggestive eyebrows frozen to my brow, that this was not very femme. Hm. Naturally Paramount Records would have photographed her in a dress. But with all of the winks, grins and grinds that must have accompanied her performances, I realized she must have been the "bull-dyke" that she was singing about.

The biographies describe how she romanced her protégée Bessie Smith, called her friends "bulldaggers" and wore her "suits like a fan." She threw sex parties at the risk of being jailed and preferred to "talk to the gals like any old man."

Gertrude "Ma" Rainey, "the Mother of the Blues," is the earliest American butch that I have ever encountered.

It is an honour to share her legacy.

One Hundred Butches

Mayhem

number thirty three

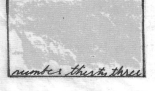

What I know about May is what I hear. Sometimes you have to go on public opinion. When I met her I thought she was unassuming. She sat privately gnawing on a baked drumstick. Shed bought a bucket of chicken for Thea's birthday and she ate it in a somehow patronly way- she delivered the meal but she didn't stand on ceremony. She chewed some thoughtfully, and then she left.

So I wasn't clear about her reputation. I was told that she was the charismatic Central Station for Arab femmes. It sounded good. One of her nicknames is Don Cliterati. "She must get exhausted by all of the attention," someone said. "No one can resist her, they're like moths to a flame."

I couldn't really grasp it, because to me she seemed stoic and restrained. I don't think we made eye contact for weeks.

Then it finally became clear to me, May is discreet for a reason: she hates to waste time. When she's in her element she's a flame-tossing, stunt-pulling darling. But some moths can't see the flame. Maybe they are narrow-minded, maybe they are preoccupied by a different fire. I'll take my cues from The Don. They are a drain. Keep to yourself, save your breath. Bide your time and enjoy yourself. Others will come, and they will be the lucky ones.

one hundred butches

thirty four

You are breaking my heart.

I'm talking, in my head, to the girl in the subway seat across from me. She probably looks a little like I do, in a half-Chinese hipster kind of way with a half-blonde haircut and blazer that screams I am so gay. As soon as she fell into that seat I thought, Hey, you're a bit like me, but younger and fancier. She was obsessively taking photographs of her straight friend because it's that late stage of the night where someone like her or I would be cheerfully clumsily drunk and compulsively admiring the girl that we're with. She was clicking photo after photo of her friend's sexy, revealing dress, her glossy, tumbling hair, her drunken explosions of laughter, and her indifferent heterosexuality, which is hardly noticeable to the untrained eye, but to any queer like us it's so obvious that this one is just obstinately straight. And if that wasn't bad enough, the straight girl has started to randomly, successfully flirt with a strange boy beside her, and now my doppelgänger is taking slower and more disheartened photographs, and saying, "Oh, let's leave this guy alone," and "why don't you come sit here next to me?"

But the girl isn't even paying attention to you anymore, because the boy is blushing and letting her snuggle with him, even though anyone can plainly see that you are the cutest plum-pie of a baby-butch-in-love ever, with the fastest-growing look of grief on your face ever, and trust me baby, I can see it all.

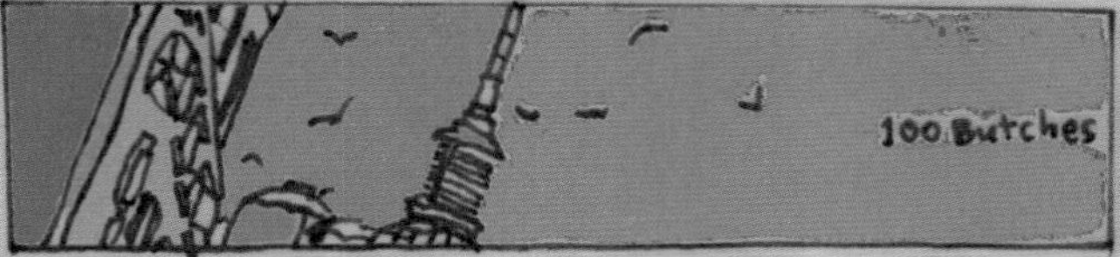

I had four hours of transit in Berlin. Two hours to pick up my stuff and two hours to get back to my connecting plane. I hadn't expected all of the delays - now I'd only get 10 minutes in her house. The old house we used to share. I don't know if I felt mad or glad.

When I transferred onto her U-Bahn line I already started to feel sick with nerves. It had been six months since I'd seen her, and the heartbreak still crushed me. I got off at the familiar exit and almost lost my breath. By the time I left the tram I realized I was shivering. My feet walked me stiffly up to number 36.

One of my old roommates opened the door, surprised to see me, two other roommates came down the stairs, and suddenly there she was. On the landing, balancing her laundry.

She leaned against the wall. She looked smaller than I remembered, but all of her features were better in real life. Her hair looked freshly cut, and her rattail still snaked around her neck. I stared at her while I gathered things and answered everyone else's questions. I had thought that she might be either cold, or friendly and indifferent, but she was herself, attentive, polite, staring, and intense.

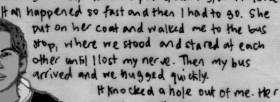

It all happened so fast and then I had to go. She put on her coat and walked me to the bus stop, where we stood and stared at each other until I lost my nerve. Then my bus arrived and we hugged quickly.

It knocked a hole out of me. Her smell, exactly the same, exactly the same, her neck, her small frame under her coat, her waist in my hand, her hand inadvertently against my breasts, that was the last thing.

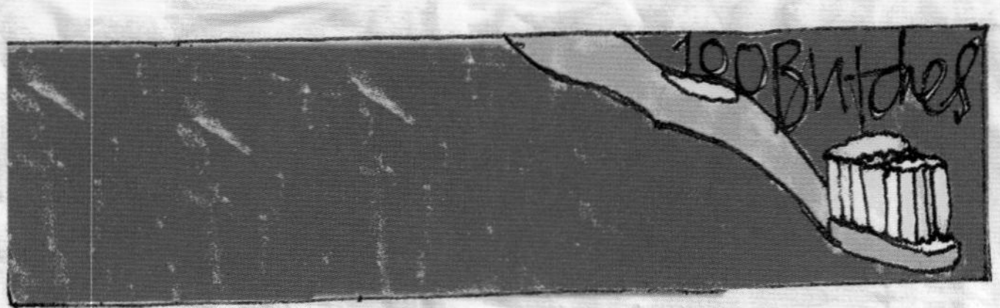
100 Butches

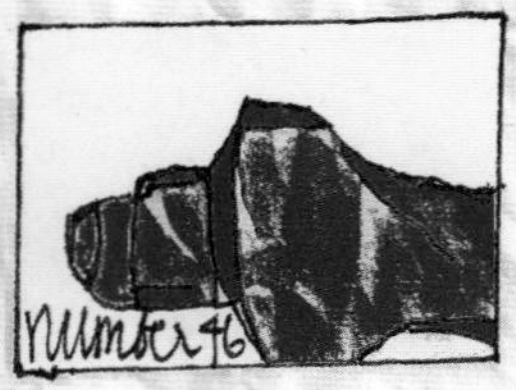
number 46

The other day my friend Aliah gave me a novel theory. She said, "You know what, if you put anyone in front of a mirror, they turn into a butch."

"What?" I said, picturing some kind of magic spell I had to learn.

"Think about it," she said. "What do people do in the mirror? They stand there pouting, right? They look at themselves and brood in total silence. Everybody does it, everybody's a thirty-second-butch in the mirror. They get all quiet and stoic and make faces like, 'Hey baby, are you lonesome tonight?'

It might be the kind of thing you only see when you're really intimate with someone," she continued. "or when they're your roommate, because it's a private thing to do. Like my ex, she's adorable. She wouldn't really call herself a butch. She's androgynous, maybe genderqueer. But there were these moments when I always thought, whoa, there's that inner butch, and it was usually when she was brushing her teeth.

"It's because she was facing a mirror! She'd stand there quietly, and watch herself from the side, and then suddenly she'd raise one eyebrow, and maybe touch up her fringe. Do you see what I'm getting at? It was hot man.'"

Then she stopped.

"I'm so gay you know. I'm a butch who likes butches." She looked at me seriously. "Is that weird?"

"Yeah," I said. "I don't hear about that a lot. It must be hard to get a date."

Which she punched me for, seeing as I'm the same way.

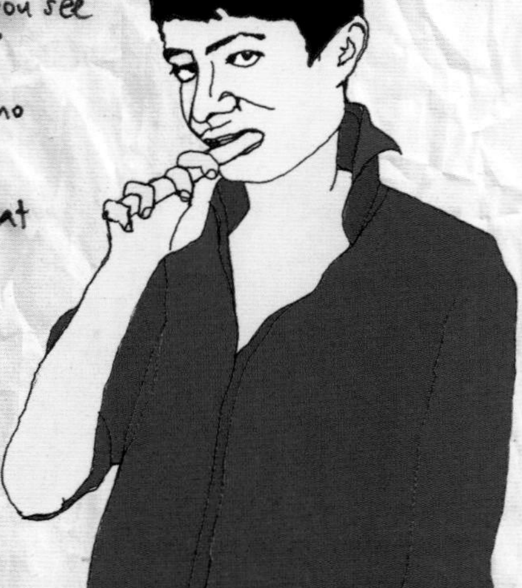

100 Butches 49

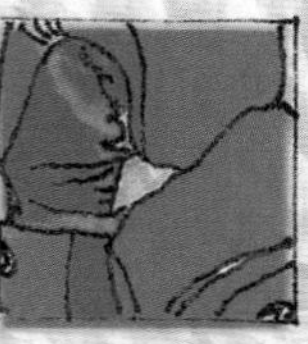

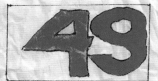

I'm so glad that Tomee decided to create a Butch/Stud support group. It's kind of amazing. Ze called it the Butch/Stud Dialogue and it's just for queer people of colour.

Some people asked why it was so closed. I wonder why it's so open. The conversations started and I quickly realized that as an East Asian butch, there is so much prejudice that I don't have to face.

I'd heard of masculine-identified folks getting kicked out of girls' bathrooms, but this was different. Members of the group shared stories about confronting new kinds of racism. "I never knew just how much discrimination Black men faced until I started to pass," someone confided. Different people described different anecdotes, about getting stopped, searched or harassed by authorities who thought that they were men. We talked about a whole new experience of hatred and fear for any queer passing as an Aboriginal, Arab or Black man.

For me, I was trying to figure out how to be a good listener. My complaints were very different.

"I disappeared," I said. "I changed from being a fetishized Chinese woman to an invisible Chinese man."

"That's something," they said, turning to me with voices full of sincerity and concern. I appreciated it, and I appreciate Tomee for creating a group that we all needed.

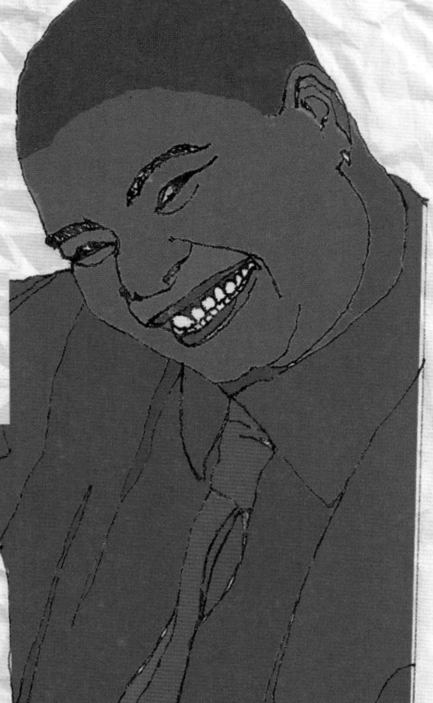

Sweetest Taboo is a
single-panel comic strip
that ran from 2009 –
2011 close to the back
page of a gay newspaper
called Capital Xtra!

Sweetest Taboo

Memoirs of a Queer Child in the Eighties

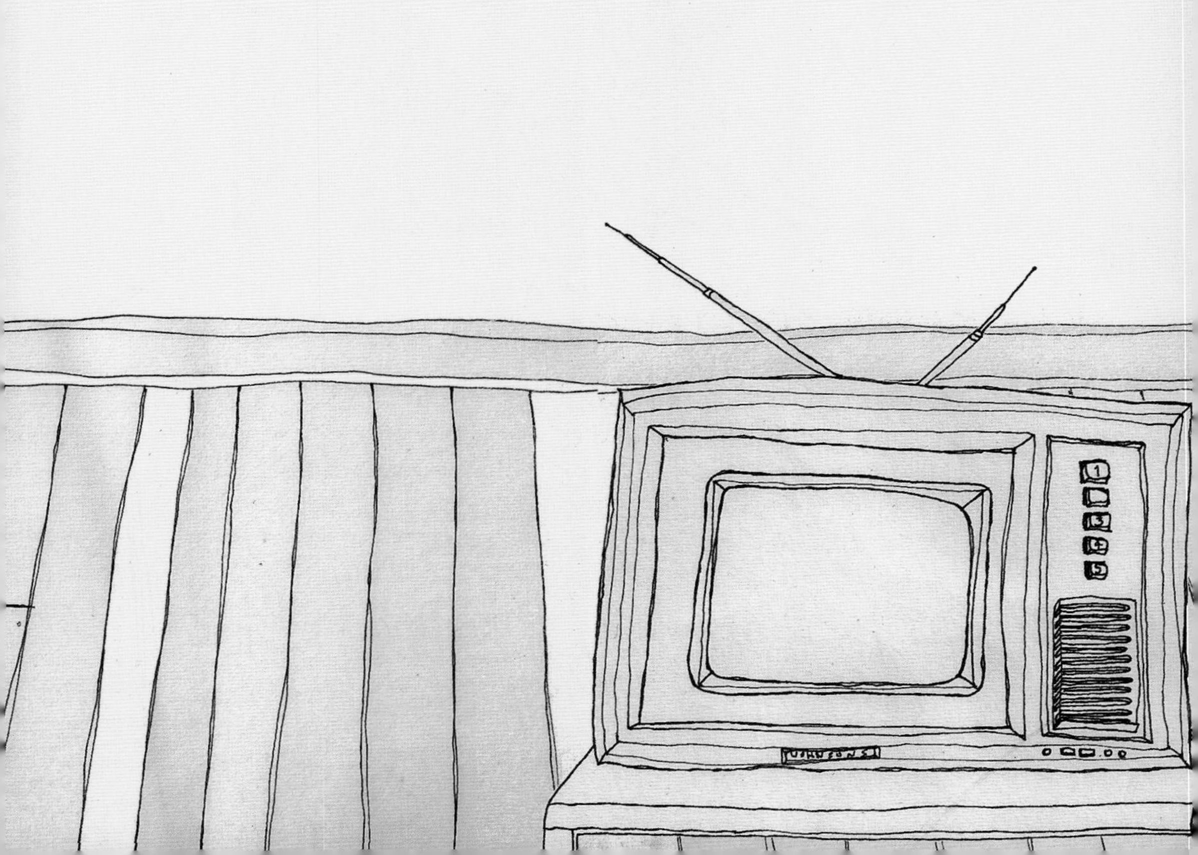

Sweetest Taboo

Memoirs of a Queer Child in the Eighties

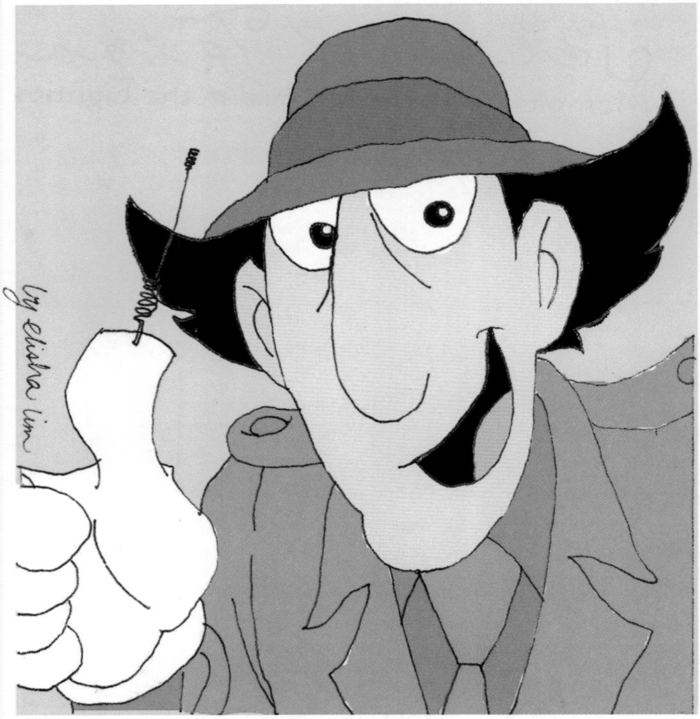
by elisha lim

Inspector Gadget was definitely a freak of nature. He had bits and bobs coming out all over his body. He had subtly erotic finger devices and a reckless, irrepressible flamboyance. No matter what he did, his niece, his niece's dog or his own clumsy accidents saved the day. He was a wonderful role model – just freakish and free.

Sweetest Taboo
Memoirs of a Queer Child in the Eighties

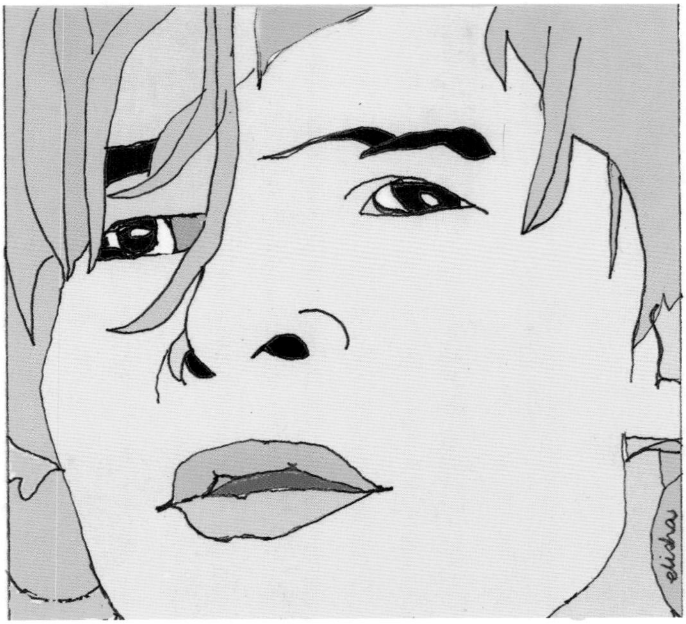
elisha

Corey Feldman. I didn't like him very much. His characters often seemed like the mean kids that would cheat you out of something on the playground. But it didn't stop my attraction. He would show up on the big screen, pull a comb out of his back pocket and comb it through his hair, and I'd feel a sudden helpless magnetism. He had something that other twelve-year-old actors didn't. Everything that he did was cunning, flirtatious and arousing. I didn't want his love, I wanted his life.

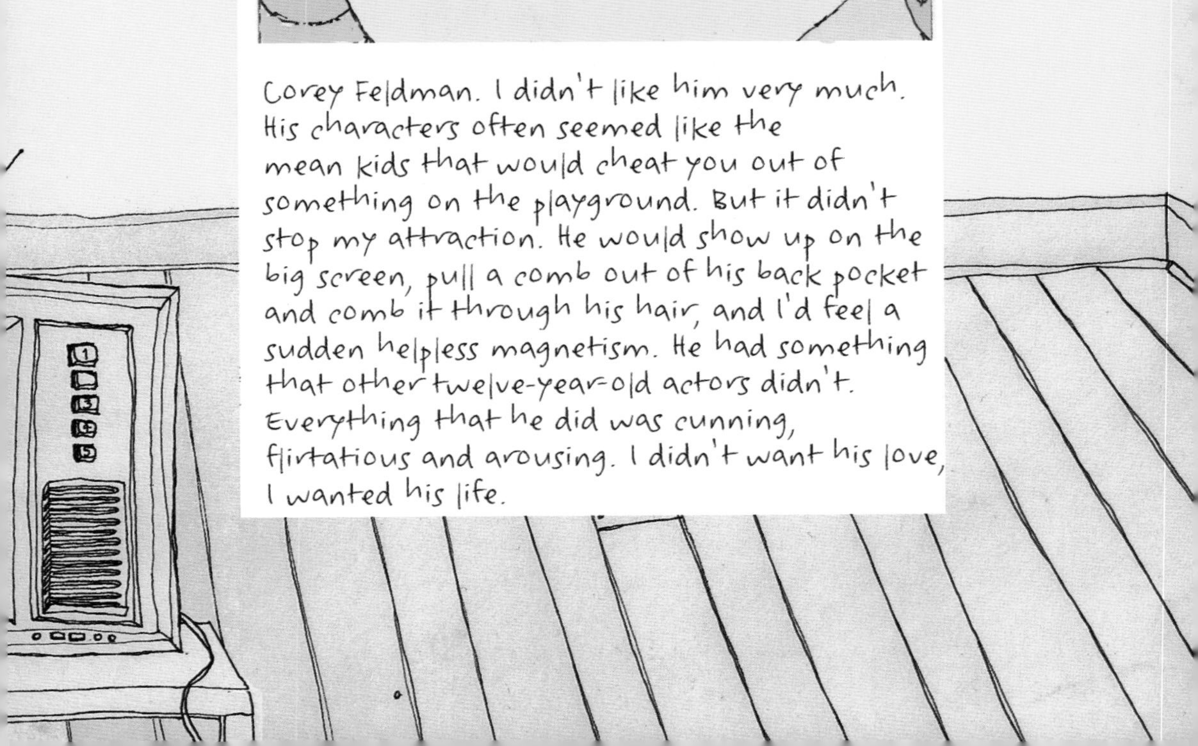

Sweetest Taboo
Memoirs of a Queer Child in the Eighties

Suddenly during the climax of Ghostbusters, the Gatekeeper and the Keymaster have passionate sex on the roof of the haunted building. I gasped. Dana Barrett is a gorgeous, feminine and elusive love interest. But when Vinz Clortho, The Keymaster, busts through the door looking for her, she swings her long leg over the armchair and agrees that she is the Gatekeeper, and then plunges him into a consuming kiss. She wasn't just any sex bomb, she was a hungry, dominant woman-monster-ghost who knew exactly what she wanted. It turned me on from my head to my toes.

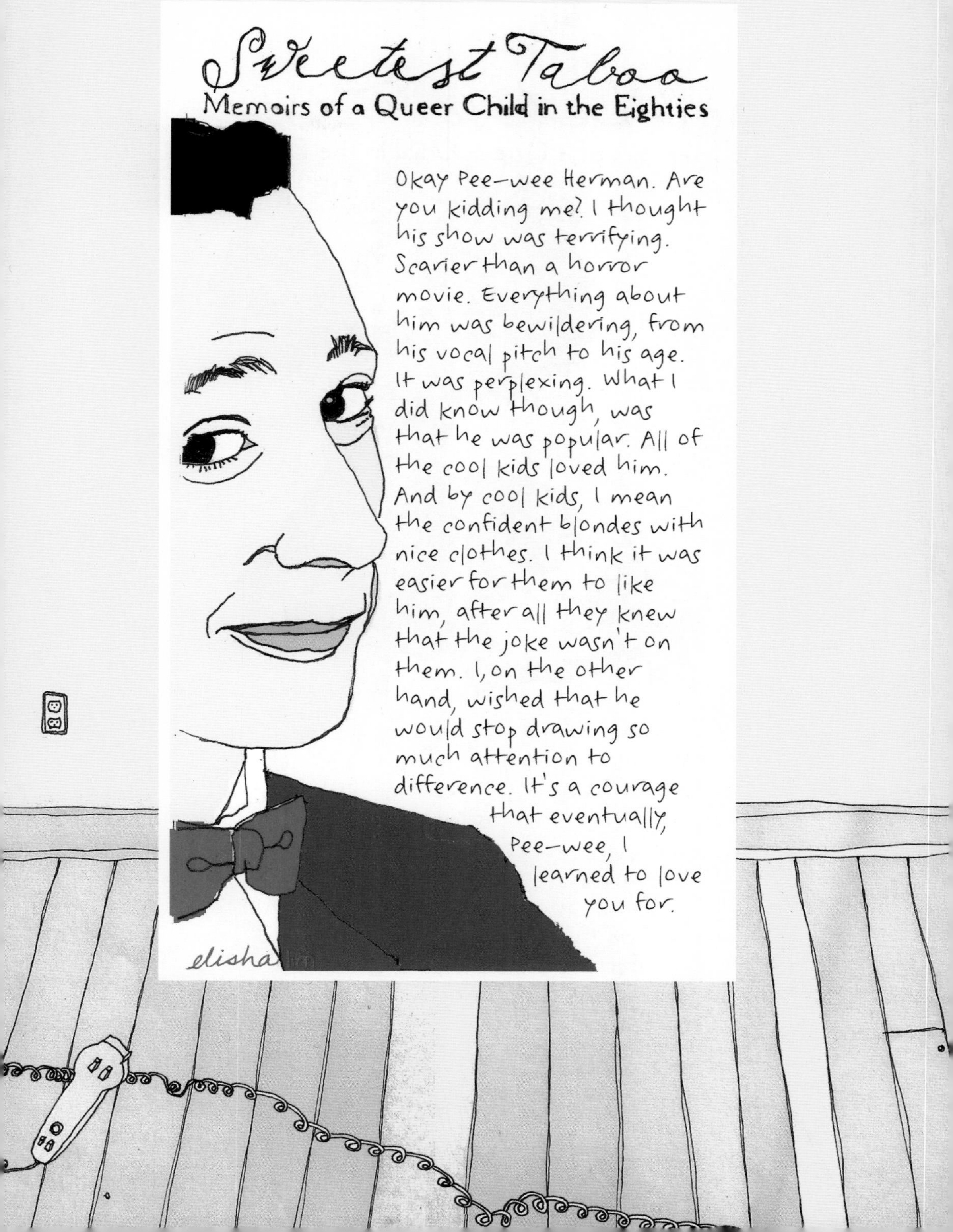
Sweetest Taboo
Memoirs of a Queer Child in the Eighties
Okay Pee-wee Herman. Are you kidding me? I thought his show was terrifying. Scarier than a horror movie. Everything about him was bewildering, from his vocal pitch to his age. It was perplexing. What I did know though, was that he was popular. All of the cool kids loved him. And by cool kids, I mean the confident blondes with nice clothes. I think it was easier for them to like him, after all they knew that the joke wasn't on them. I, on the other hand, wished that he would stop drawing so much attention to difference. It's a courage that eventually, Pee-wee, I learned to love you for.
elisha

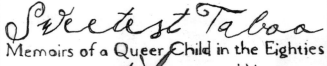

Sweetest Taboo
Memoirs of a Queer Child in the Eighties

I actually found Fraggle Rock pretty intimidating. Maybe it was too athletic for an awkward bookworm. But in any case, there was this lead girl fraggle called Red, and she had attitude and an androgynous body and she seemed to be in charge. She was a girl character, but she didn't wear makeup or heels like Smurfette or Miss Piggy. She was just a little genderqueer furball and everybody still loved her.

Sweetest Taboo

Memoirs of a Queer Child in the Eighties

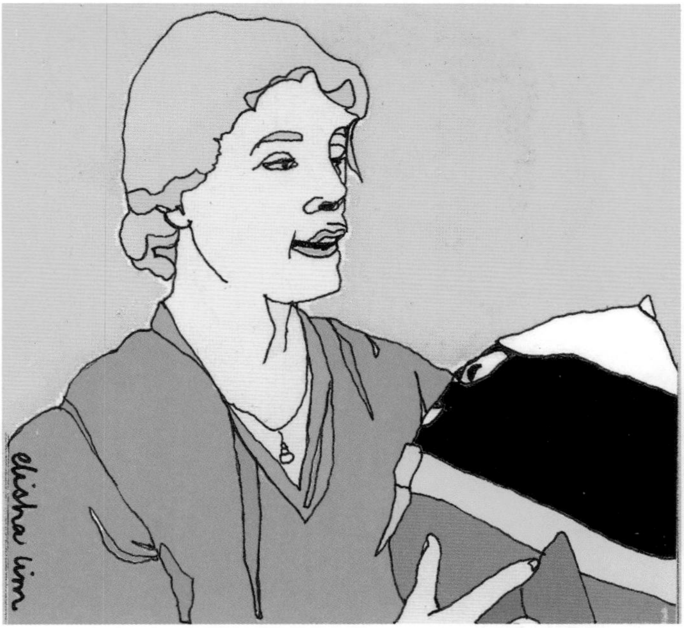
elisha lim

I hear that the male hosts of Polka Dot Door dressed effeminately in order to appear less threatening to children. I found that extremely threatening. They were not like the men on every other channel. Who were these perverts in high, tight velour pants, I wanted to know? It made me feel wary and suspicious. I credit Polka Dot Door for blowing a hole in some of my stricter young gender definitions.

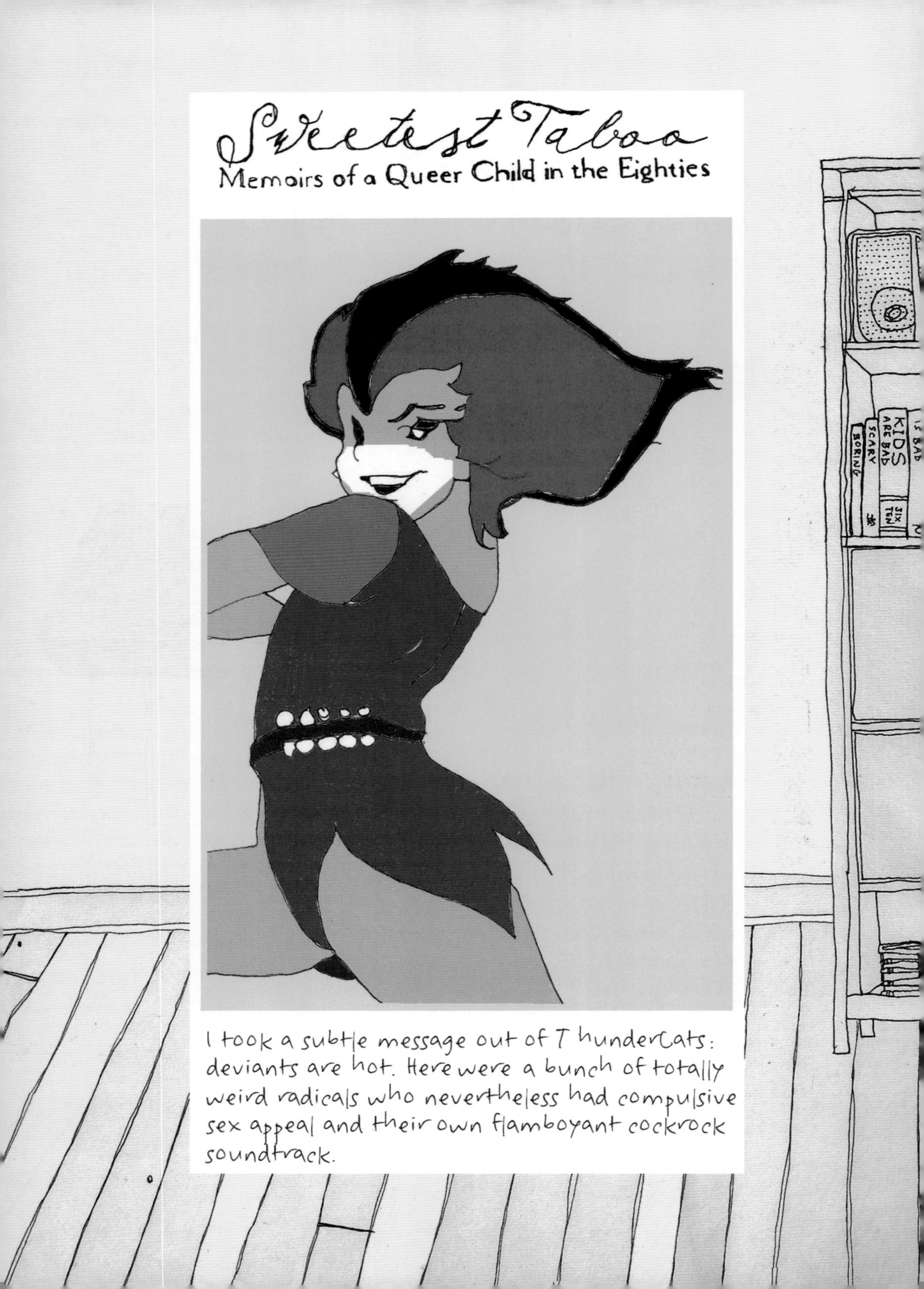
Sweetest Taboo
Memoirs of a Queer Child in the Eighties
BORING
SCARY
KIDS ARE BAD
IS BAD
SIX TEN
I took a subtle message out of Thundercats: deviants are hot. Here were a bunch of totally weird radicals who nevertheless had compulsive sex appeal and their own flamboyant cockrock soundtrack.

Sweetest Taboo

Memoirs of a Queer Child in the Eighties

PICTURES THAT MAKE NO SENSE
GROSS
SEX IS GREAT
BORING

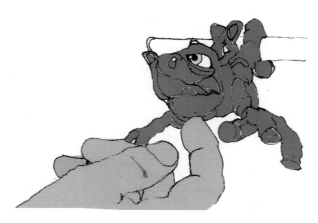

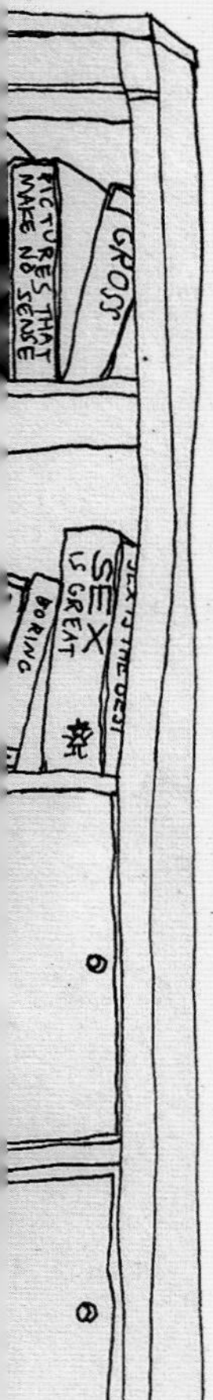

In my memory eighties' movie plots are full of impossible erotic attractions between humans and non-humans. It was gripping in the Flight of the Navigator when David bonded with a little fist-sized fuzzy creature. At one point he accidentally crushes it under his hand because it's just a big squeaky caterpillar. But he flirts and tickles and falls in love with it, even though it has the eighties-special-effects realism of fungus. He couldn't be parted with his oddly repulsive little companion, and he eventually smuggles it home to Earth. I realize that this wasn't intended to be sexual, but I was intoxicated by it, and so many other peculiar and wonderfully transgressive couplings, all decade.

Sweetest Taboo
Memoirs of a Queer Child in the Eighties

WEIRD NEIGHBOURS

Sharon, Lois & Bram were lovely. One nice man and one nice lady...and then one more nice lady. I decided that they were all married together. Everything fit in strict categories in my child's mind. Sets of female and male adults must be married. And in the case of Sharon, Lois & Bram, they must be in a three-way marriage... and that must be a normal thing.

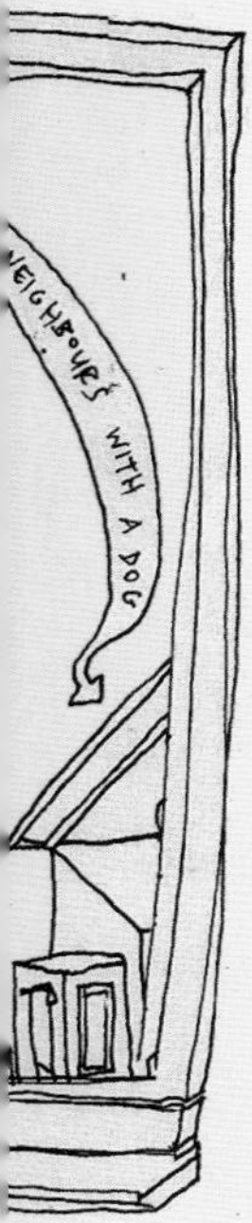
NEIGHBOURS WITH A DOG

Sweetest Taboo

Memoirs of a Queer Child in the Eighties

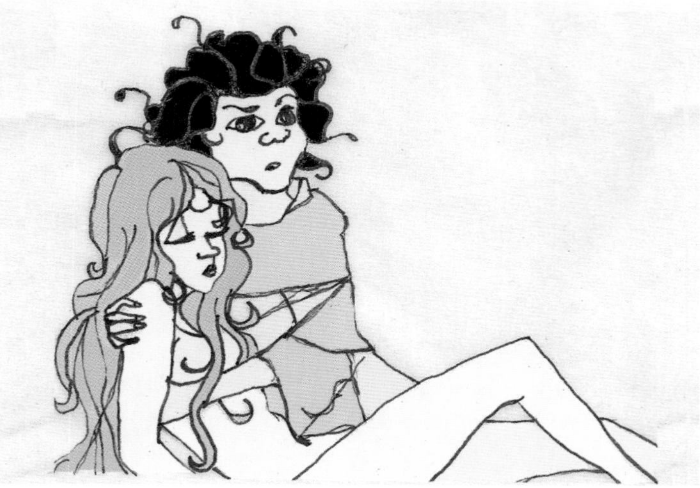

The Last Unicorn was just a scandal. Everything about it was a cryptic queer code. One of the moments that impressed my young mind was when the Unicorn was magically turned into a woman. She, Molly Grue and I were all aghast. My young butch sensibilities were particularly disturbed. She was altered from a spirited beast into a naked, nubile, hyper-feminized sex object. What misfortune! What injustice to be forced to be a woman against your will! At least, that's what I thought.

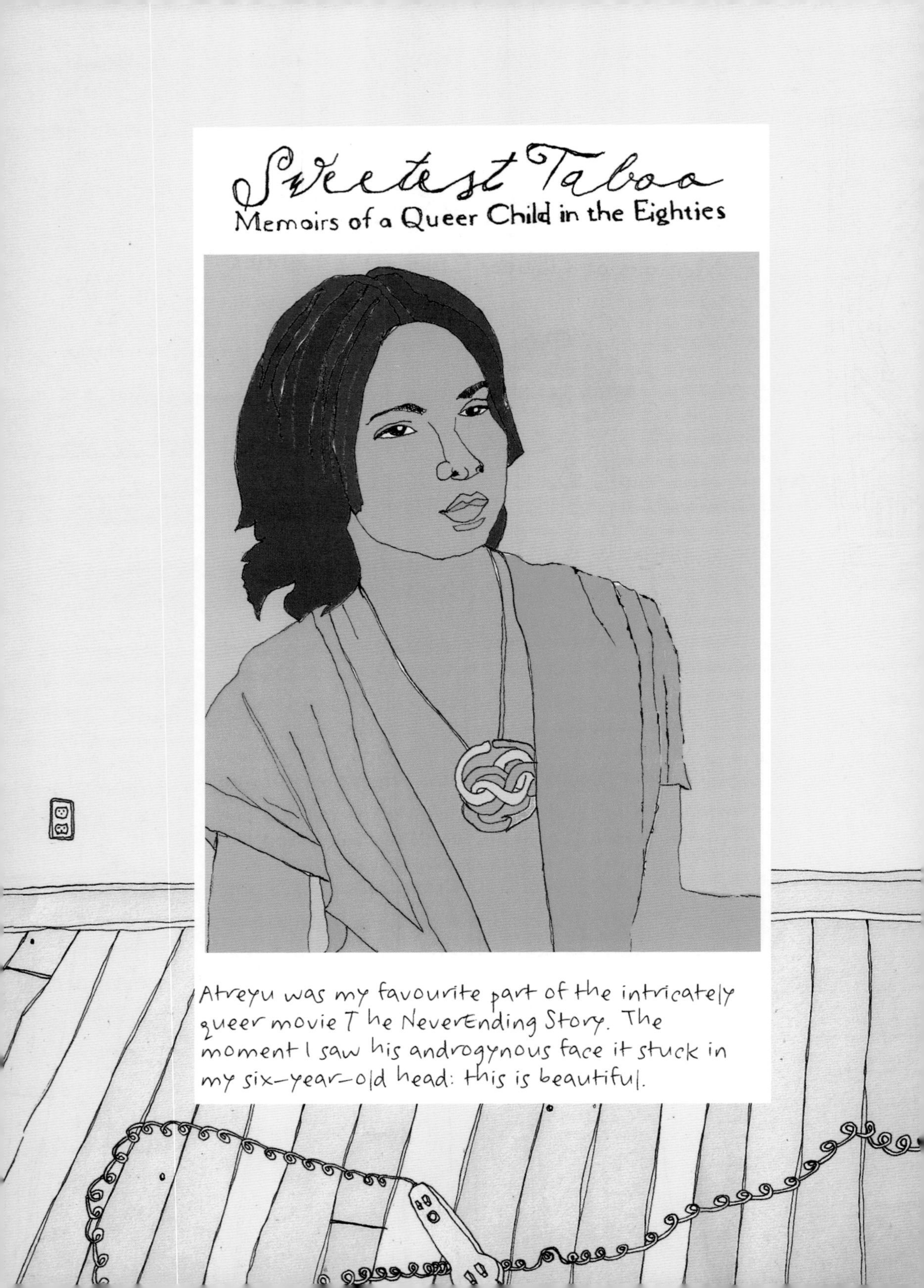
Sweetest Taboo
Memoirs of a Queer Child in the Eighties
Atreyu was my favourite part of the intricately queer movie The NeverEnding Story. The moment I saw his androgynous face it stuck in my six-year-old head: this is beautiful.

Sweetest Taboo

Memoirs of a Queer Child in the Eighties

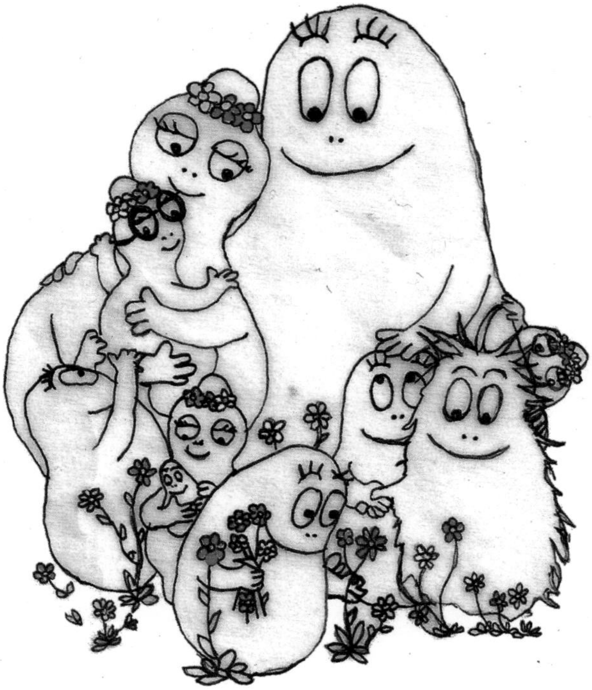

In a world where horniness felt like an inexplicable itch and masturbation seemed to be something that I'd invented, the elastic, unpredictable, permissive, shapeless romantic world of the Barbapapas and Barbamamas made it seem like nothing could be "wrong," and anything could be "right."

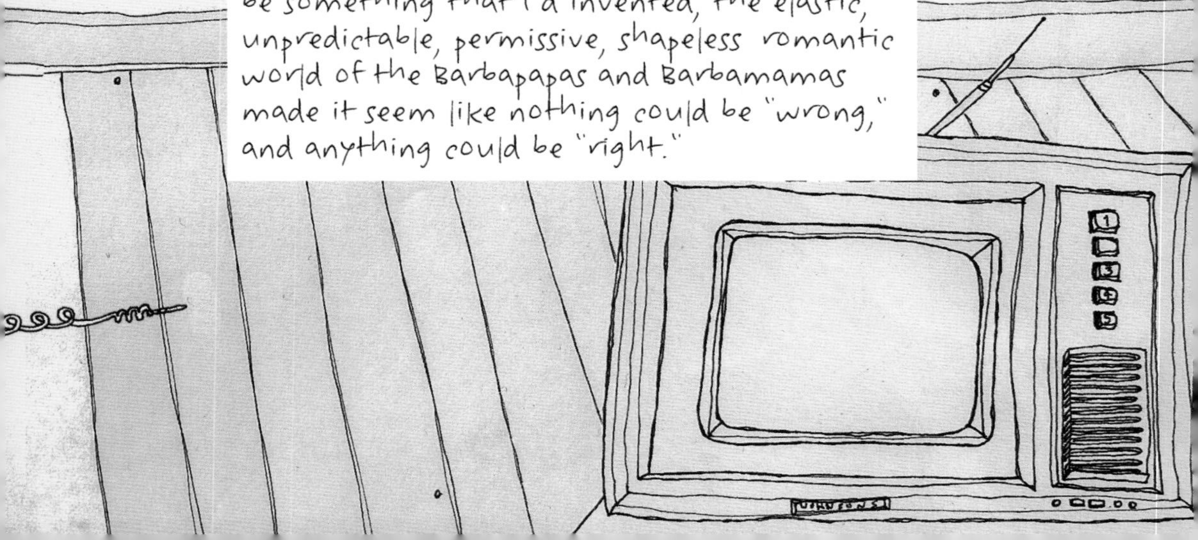

I was in a bookstore one night poring over a beautiful men's fashion book called something like "The Illustrated Gentleman." I felt a mix of pleasure and pain, thinking that none of these dashing outfits would fit me right, and that I couldn't afford them anyway.

My solution was to start a butch fashion zine.

Maybe we couldn't afford our dream outfits, but I could draw portraits of us trying them on in the change room, giving each other tips, talking about our fashion heroes and documenting the queer friendliness of each clothing store. It would be our own illustrated book of subversive sartorial splendour.

The Illustrated Gentleman

disha

The Illustrated Gentleman

disha

When we went into the Montreal chain, Eshan's first impulse was to touch the argyle sweater vests. Handsome seaters in yellow, black and orange matched up deliciously next to blazing citrus ties.

It was a men's store but the assistant made us feel pretty comfortable. She acted as if it was totally normal that we were in there, and she didn't ask if we were shopping for someone else. When we picked up

a tie she even asked if she could help make it into a Windsor knot.
Eshan finally fell in love with a tie in shiny, rippling black-and-red pinstripes, with a grey vest and a white shirt.

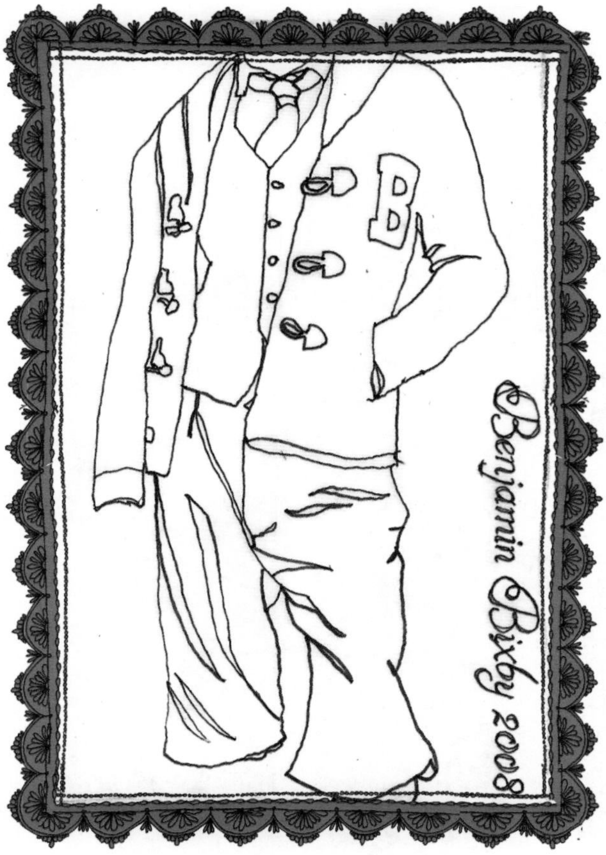
B
Benjamin Bixby 2008

One of my favourite fashion tales is the story of Andre 3000. He's a very deliberate dandy, and started off showing up at Outkast photo shoots with bags full of extra outfits in order to develop his reputation. It worked. In 2004 Esquire called him "the world's best-dressed man."

He described his Atlanta high school 'prep crew.' "It was all about being a prep," he said. "It was about ties and saddle shoes and Guess overalls and stuff like that." His style was inspired by period pieces like 'The Great Gatsby' and old men in his neighbourhood.

So you can imagine my thrill to learn that he had reinvented himself as a fashion designer, without any training or background. His line 'Benjamin Bixby' is based on "images, drawn from college football circa 1935," after a documentary he stumbled across on TV one night.

"For an African-American guy to be a prep, that's a dichotomy," he says. "Prep style comes from mostly affluent families who just wear these cool clothes. But when you come from a background that has more struggle, your take on it will be different. There's a certain kind of rebel to it."

Cynthia and I went to a prestigious suit shop in Toronto's Kensington Market. As soon as we walked in we were told to find the women's clothes on the left. The clerks tried to discourage us from climbing the stairs to the men's section.

Upstairs we were largely ignored. I asked a clerk, loudly, if there were any jackets that might fit me. I wanted to spare Cynthia the embarrassment. He looked at us.

"Fit who?" he asked, until we repeated ourselves. He answered, "you want a women's jacket."

"No," we said, "we want a man's jacket."

"Well," he said, "if I had to give you a jacket what would I do with the pants? Men's pants would be too small for your hips."

"Yes," I agreed. "Could you find me a pair that would fit?"

"What?" he cried. "And destroy a suit? If I separate a fitted jacket and pant set that would destroy a suit! I'm not going to destroy a suit."

Afterwards Cynthia didn't know what else to do but laugh. "He was beside himself," she said. "He must have said 'destroy' three times."

Cynthia is posing in a suit to replicate her grandfather.

"In Hong Kong," she told me, "he was an old school gentleman, like with an umbrella and a cane. My mum tells the story that his friends were pretty rich and would help his family out. Later on they lost their money and he always gave back to them.

What makes you classy is how you carry yourself, and treat other people. It's how you respect people. I didn't know him well, but these are the values that he passed down. I hope he isn't turning over in his grave though, and saying 'oh my god my granddaughter is a cross-dresser.'

"I like wearing a suit," she continued. "I wish my body could fit it better though, and I wish it was more acceptable. I wish it didn't look like I was just trying to get attention. It would be nice if people would simply say, 'you're really looking dapper today.'

"You know, once I went on a date in a suit," she smiled. "My date was wearing a dress, and I thought to myself, well this is her fancy get-up, and this is my fancy get-up. And this is a great evening."

Michèle shows up at parties in perfect matching baby blue shirts and boat shoes. It's too good. She tells me that it's been a really long time since she's felt uncomfortable shopping in the men's section. Other people's reactions used to bother her, so she would make slight concessions to try and fit in a little better to avoid the drama, like shopping in the men's section in a mixed department store, but avoiding strictly men's stores.

Now she really doesn't care. "I'm much more comfortable in my body than I used to be," she says, "which has really changed the way that I dress and the way that I shop." Her style has evolved over the past few years. "These days I'm all about fit," she says. She delightfully describes her look as half dyke / half fag. "I guess you could also say that I'm a bit of a dandy sometimes."

One of my favourite stylists is Shanieke "Shin" Peru. I've always loved watching macho music videos and thinking, "I can dress like that." But you know I don't turn out looking like the chiselled picture of Lil Wayne. I turn out looking more like a chubby homosexual. So I felt so gratified to learn about Shin. She's the artist that Black male celebrities turn to, including Usher, Ne-Yo, Nas, Kevin Liles and Jamie Foxx. Most thrillingly, she describes her personal taste as androgynous and inconsistent. "I love mixing masculine and feminine... I get excited taking the most masculine article of clothing and transforming it into something sexy."

It blows me away to realize that I'm not only trying to emulate Ne-Yo. I'm trying to emulate you, Shin, so thank you.

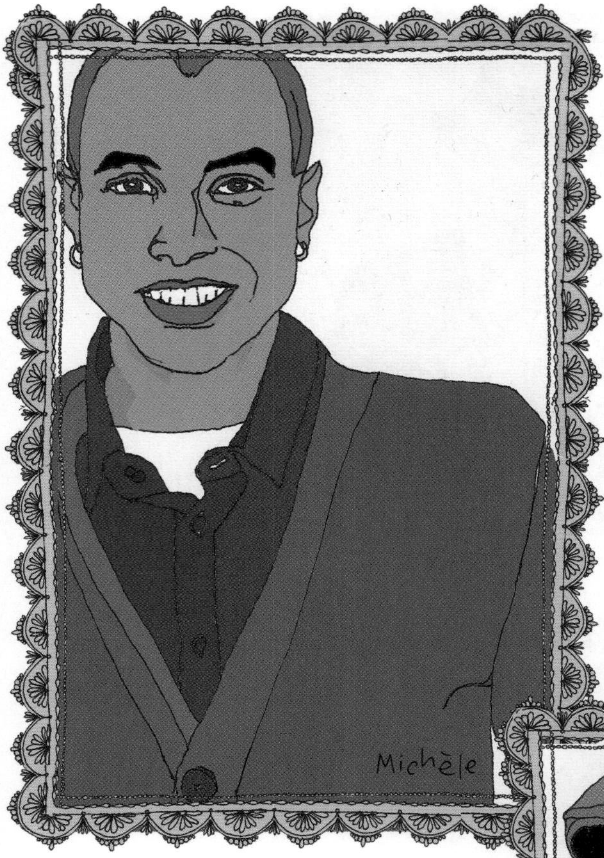
Michèle

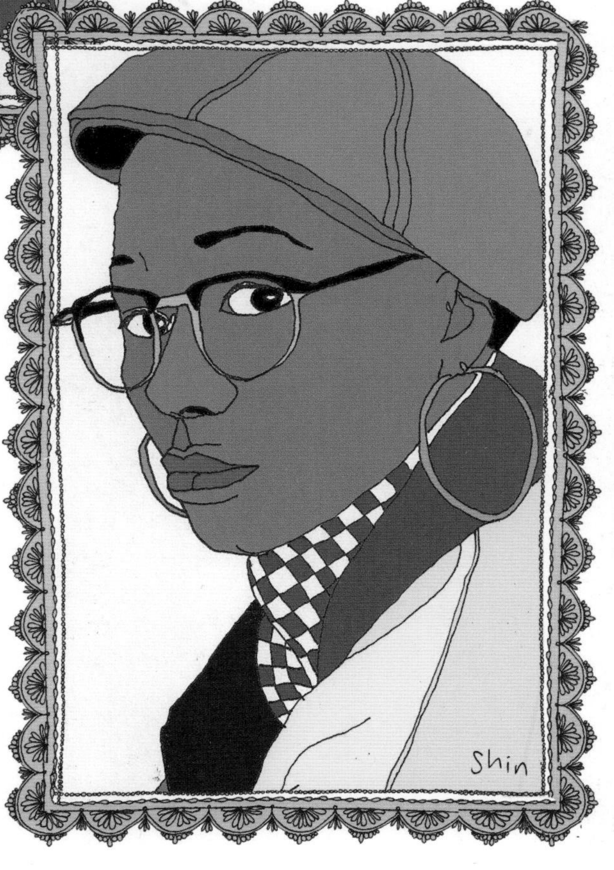
Shin

Laura doesn't feel awkward in the men's section at all. "If I feel uncomfortable anywhere," she says, "it's in the women's section. In the someone's section I think, What are people thinking when they look at me? What sort of questions do I need to ask here?"

These are some of Laura's rules to outfitting. "Boxer briefs are essential," she says. "They're a gentleman's bra. They squeeze and uplift your ass. Other than that. a great watch and great shoes."

snug shoulders

butch fashion icon j. shimizu

cup the jacket

For me the hardest thing about suit shopping is an intimidating shopping trip. So I took a survey for some tips to be as informed, confident and entitled as any cis guy might be. The best advice came from my femme friends.

Farrah said, "shop for a vintage or secondhand suit and then take it to a tailor. Make sure you try it on again before paying."

Ladan said, "make sure the shoulders hug yours."

Jiating said, "you should be able to hold the bottom of the jacket and there shouldn't be more than a fist–length of space between the buttons and your binder."

Nadia said, "show a bit of sleeve. And double vents are in right now."

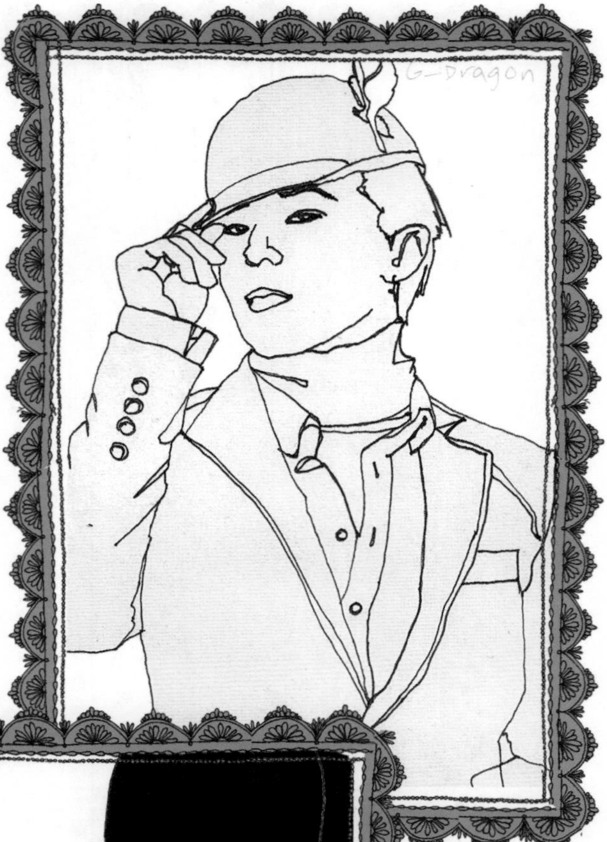
G-Dragon

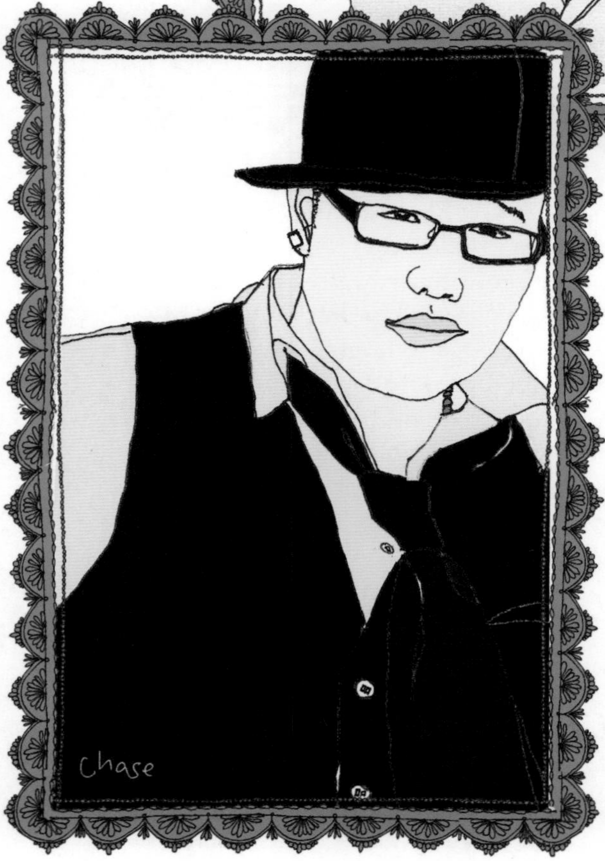
Chase

Chase describes his style as GQ casual. He says,
"Since I started identifying as trans I've become
meticulous about how my clothes fit. But I notice that
when I shop I'm either ignored or scrutinized because
clerks assume that I don't have money to spend, or that
I'm a criminal. Banana Republic staff don't pay me any
attention and H&M becomes vigilant as soon as I walk in.

Chase's fashion role model is G-Dragon "because he
doesn't even try to compete with white heteronormative
masculinity.
"East Asian men are a last choice as North American male
role models, stereotyped as submissive, inscrutable and
effeminate. So East Asian queers have to face a secondary
racist hurdle in order to produce credible male sex appeal.
"Many Korean pop stars model themselves off of White or
Black masculinity but G-Dragon flaunts his own
emasculated homoerotic brand of appeal and he has
succeeded in becoming an iconic Korean pop sex symbol.
He wears makeup, earrings and tight tapered outfits, and
he doesn't waste time on biceps or a six pack. He
brandishes subversive sex appeal and paves the way for
atypical Asian masculinity."

I was shopping with my dad at a chain boutique with a french name. "But these are men's clothes," he was saying in a pained voice, "I don't understand what you would want with them." We drifted through the store in our private griefs. By the time the store clerk approached me, I was alone in the men's section. I was self-conscious about it — the men's and women's sections were totally separate. Even the entrances were separate. But she put me at ease. "Great choice of sweaters," she said sincerely as I tried on a red sweater over a black shirt and red satin tie. So I gave it a shot and asked her a question.

"It's pretty gender-segregated in here, isn't it?" I said.

She looked at me and lowered her voice. "They explicitly forbid me from modelling men's clothes she confided. "I get less of a staff discount on men's clothes. I'm not even allowed to wear a tie. But the worst thing," she whispered, "is the other staff. I've heard them freak out just because a guy wanted to try on a pair of heels."

We looked at each other sadly. I thought she was terrific, but my defences went up, and I started to put things shyly back on the shelf.

One Christmas my family had assembled, as usual, in a hotel room somewhere between our many far-flung continents. We'd dumped our presents on the bed and were trying to make the best of cheerfully unwrapping them. My sister passed one over to me. "To Elisha From Daddy," it said on a long, soft rectangle. I started squeezing and tearing at it when I suddenly realized what it was. I was so overwhelmed that to my embarrassment I started to cry. Tears fell quietly down my face faster than I could wipe them away. It was a tie. When I opened it, it wasn't just any tie, it was the perfect tie. It was shiny and black and sheathed in lace, like a sissy butch dream. I stood in the corner of the room petting it foolishly. It meant so very much to me. I wondered if my dad even realized how much. It was definitely my taste in clothes. But more than that, it was a gesture of his love for me, the secret, real, butch me.

I stumbled over and hugged him. "Thank you," I stuttered. It was all I could think of, and it wasn't enough. There was such a lifetime of words that I wanted to say to him: That I had been sad for so long I didn't even realize anymore, that I had distanced myself from him out of fear, that I was so scared and shy, but ready to meet him halfway. Instead I just kept saying "thank you," awkwardly, embarrassingly and wholeheartedly.

SISSY was inspired by conversations and Tumblrs about jewellery. I noticed that I wasn't the only guy into lacey fluttery dangling necklaces — other masculine queers showed off pretty accessories in scrolling photos and even talked about their femme identities. It fit me so well that I decided to make a comic about the phenomenon. I posted on Facebook:

September 8, 2011
hayyy! I'm looking for queers of colour who'd like to model for my next calendar. I'm looking for anyone who relates to the word SISSY. Do you? Does anyone you know? xoxoxoxoxoxo!
I didn't get the response I'd expected, which was exciting. 'Sissy' as an identity appealed to dandy bois like me, but also to gay men and femmes. I also met people who disliked the word and wanted to talk about that. I love to record queer culture, not only by my stories, but by the complicated debates and conversations of the people around me.

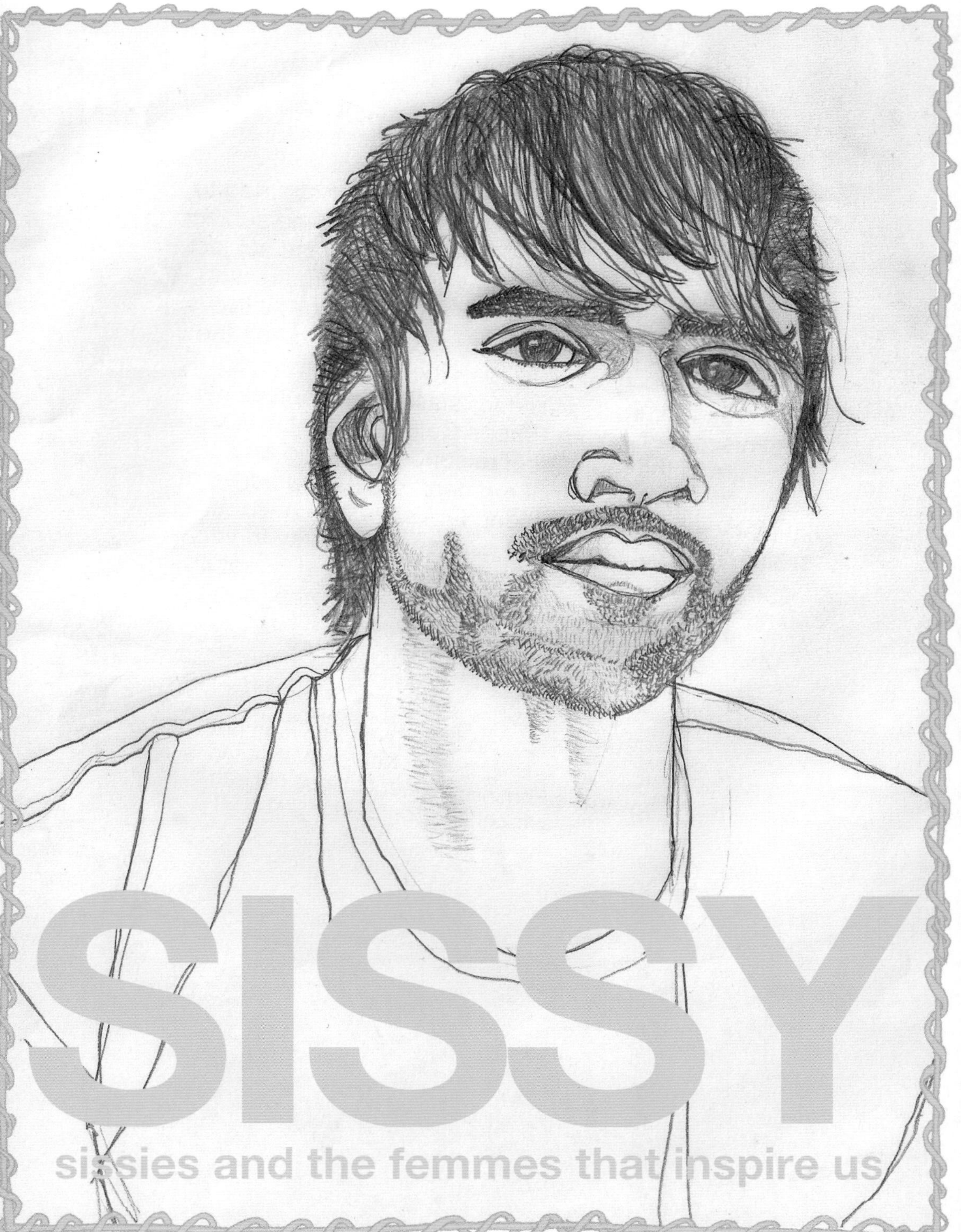

SISSY

sissies and the femmes that inspire us

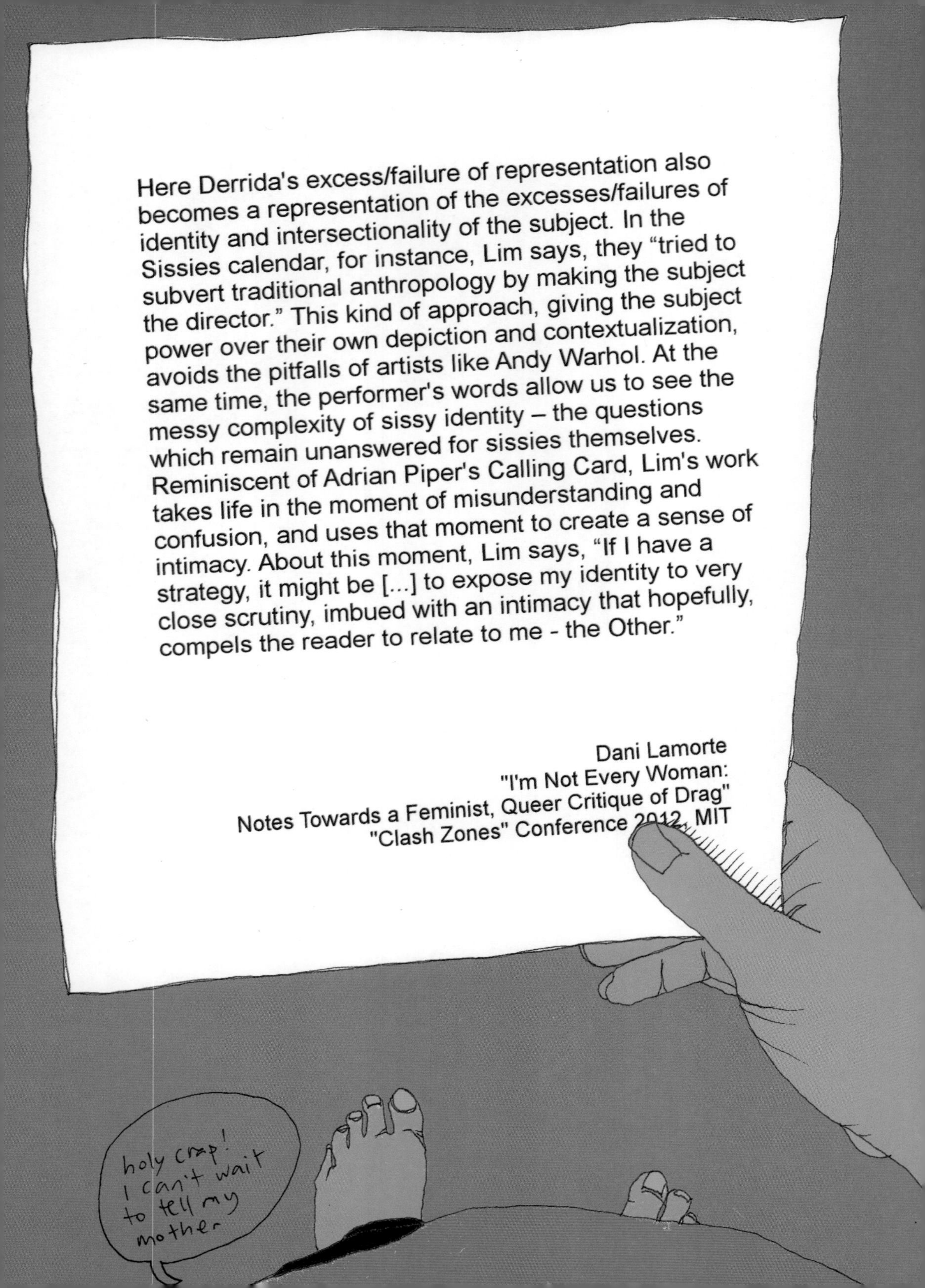

Here Derrida's excess/failure of representation also becomes a representation of the excesses/failures of identity and intersectionality of the subject. In the Sissies calendar, for instance, Lim says, they "tried to subvert traditional anthropology by making the subject the director." This kind of approach, giving the subject power over their own depiction and contextualization, avoids the pitfalls of artists like Andy Warhol. At the same time, the performer's words allow us to see the messy complexity of sissy identity – the questions which remain unanswered for sissies themselves. Reminiscent of Adrian Piper's Calling Card, Lim's work takes life in the moment of misunderstanding and confusion, and uses that moment to create a sense of intimacy. About this moment, Lim says, "If I have a strategy, it might be [...] to expose my identity to very close scrutiny, imbued with an intimacy that hopefully, compels the reader to relate to me - the Other."

Dani Lamorte
"I'm Not Every Woman:
Notes Towards a Feminist, Queer Critique of Drag"
"Clash Zones" Conference 2012, MIT

holy crap! I can't wait to tell my mother

kama

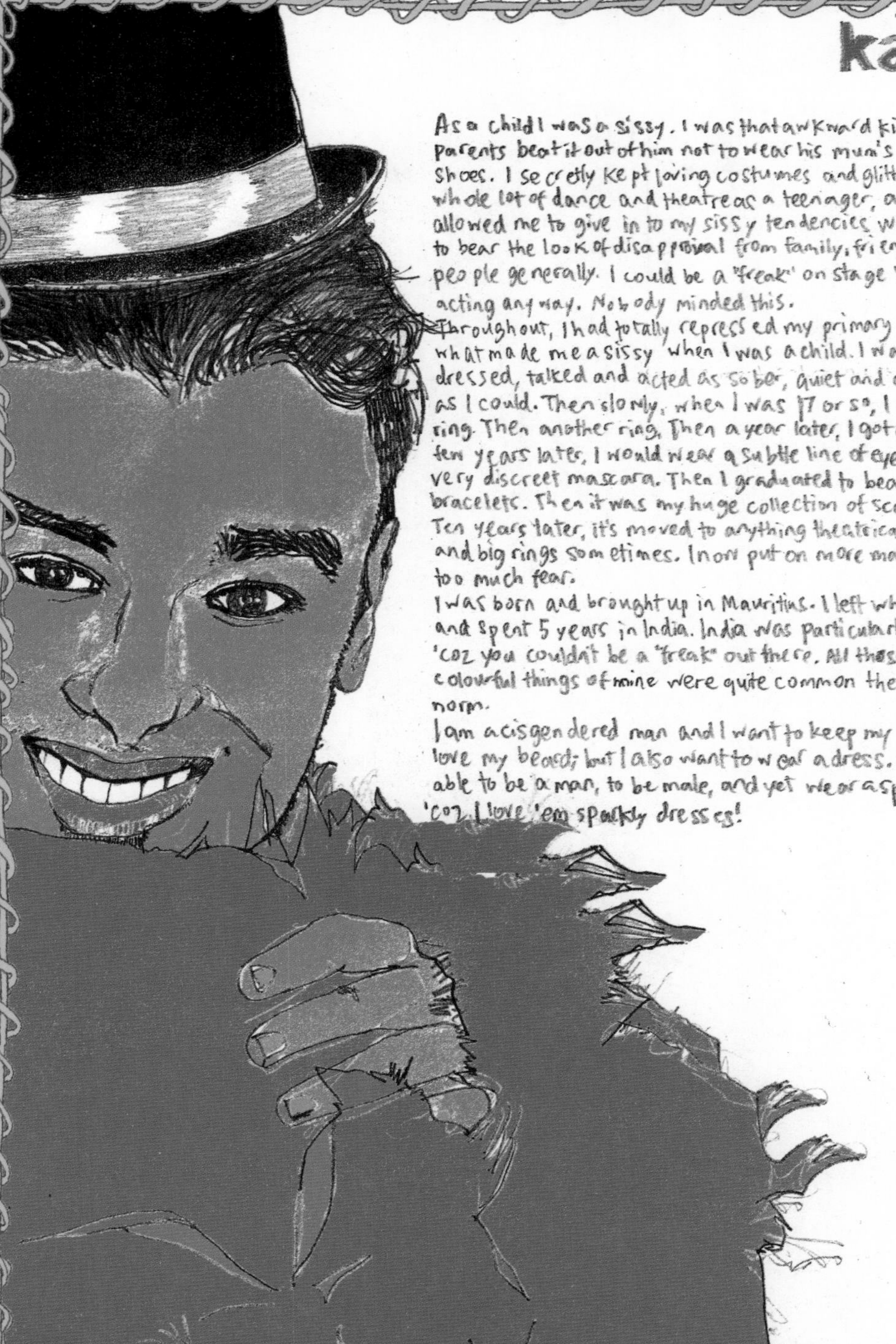

As a child I was a sissy. I was that awkward kid whose parents beat it out of him not to wear his mum's clothes and shoes. I secretly kept loving costumes and glitter. I did a whole lot of dance and theatre as a teenager, and this allowed me to give in to my sissy tendencies without having to bear the look of disapproval from family, friends and people generally. I could be a "freak" on stage 'coz I was just acting anyway. Nobody minded this.

Throughout, I had totally repressed my primary attraction to what made me a sissy when I was a child. I walked, dressed, talked and acted as sober, quiet and conventional as I could. Then slowly, when I was 17 or so, I wore a thumb ring. Then another ring. Then a year later, I got a piercing. A few years later, I would wear a subtle line of eye-liner. And very discreet mascara. Then I graduated to beads and bracelets. Then it was my huge collection of scarves. Ten years later, it's moved to anything theatrical, to big hats and big rings sometimes. I now put on more make up without too much fear.

I was born and brought up in Mauritius. I left when I was 18 and spent 5 years in India. India was particularly exciting 'coz you couldn't be a "freak" out there. All those sissy and colourful things of mine were quite common there, almost the norm.

I am a cisgendered man and I want to keep my beard 'coz I love my beard; but I also want to wear a dress. I want to be able to be a man, to be male, and yet wear a sparkly dress 'coz I love 'em sparkly dresses!

frau muttermund

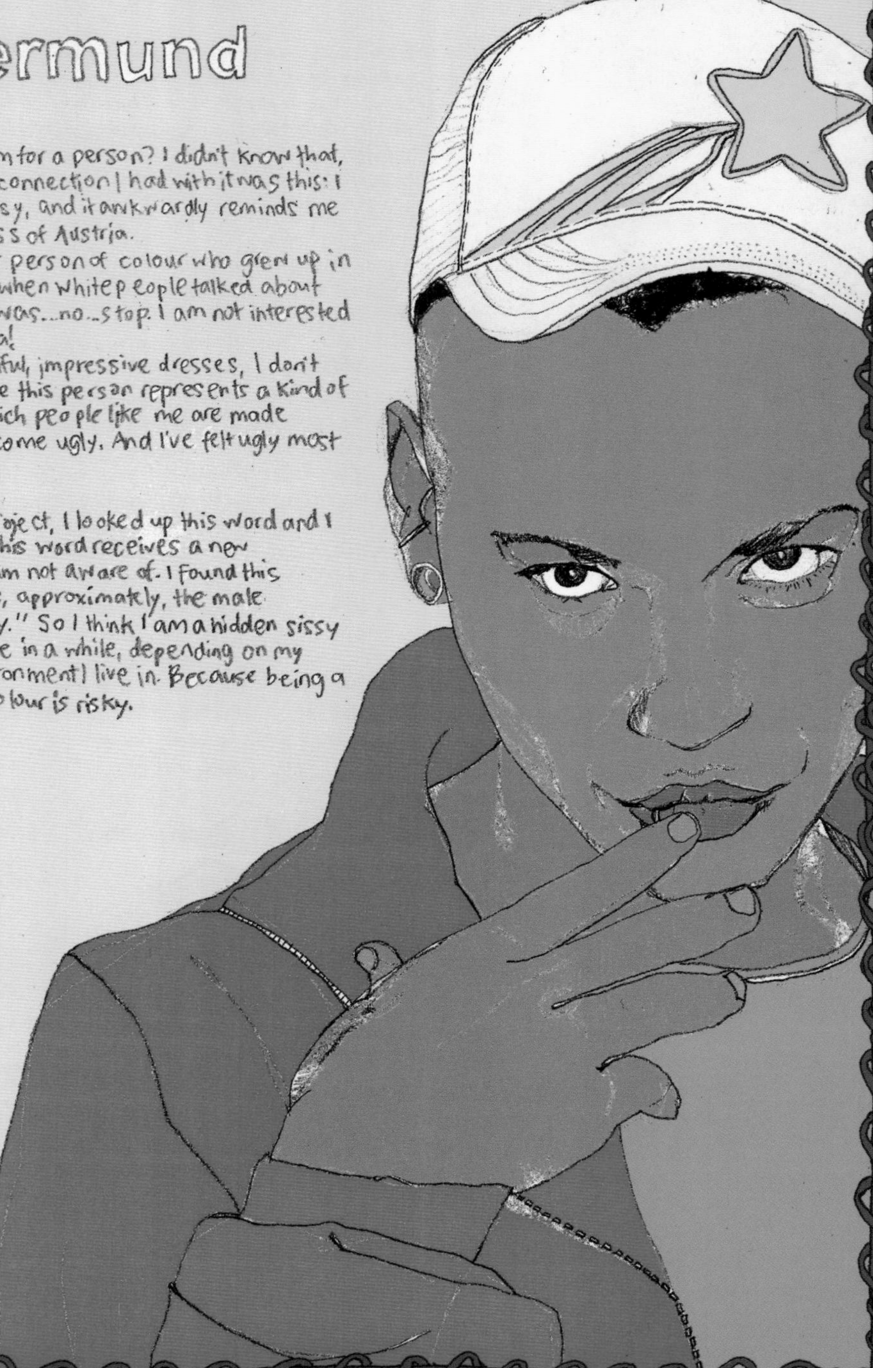

Sissy – that's a term for a person? I didn't know that, honestly. The first connection I had with it was this: I know the name sissy, and it awkwardly reminds me of the white empress of Austria.
I am a transqueer person of colour who grew up in East Germany so when white people talked about sissy all I thought was... no.. stop. I am not interested in your sissy-mania!
So - besides beautiful, impressive dresses, I don't like sissy. Because this person represents a kind of beauty through which people like me are made invisible or just become ugly. And I've felt ugly most of my life.

But now, for this project, I looked up this word and I am surprised that this word receives a new connotation that I am not aware of. I found this sentence: "Sissy is, approximately, the male converse of tomboy." So I think I am a hidden sissy that comes out once in a while, depending on my mood and the environment I live in. Because being a visible "sissy"-of-colour is risky.

sissy inspiration!
erika

Erika never fails to delight my sissy side. When I am rich I will pay her to buy my wardrobe. This is what she tells me:

When masculine queers wear feminine things it makes me feel many complicated things - depending on the specific flavour (raced, classed) of masculinity/femininity being performed, the person's gender, and the intent behind it. It's definitely amazing when people don't feel pressured to perform super binary genders, but it's sometimes frustrating when people are like "that's cool on transgressive (i.e. masculine) folks, but not cool on women," as though femininity and/or femmeness are inherently boring and regressive on women and need masculinity or men to validate them. (This affects both cis and trans women, but especially trans women, who get policed in much more awful ways than I have been!) Yet I'm also really happy to see any people expressing radical femininity and femmeness and not being censured for it by their/our communities.

I have lots of stockings, and I always shop with a palette in mind: blacks, greys and darker colours. I took a good look in the mirror and decided what colours work for me. Pastels and weak colours don't. It's also good to keep an eye on other total babes who look like me, with the same body type and skin colour - because what looks good on them might look good on me. Welovecolors.com has good selection, quality and sizing, and might be an easy way for queers to shop discreetly. There's also a fetish store called Il Bolero that seems to be pro-gender bending and they have the most beautiful selection of stockings - it's on St Hubert south of Jean-Talon.

I also love having fucking gigantic clouds of hair. It feels like the embodiment of femme to me - natural, yet highly cultivated. It's also not the way Black women are supposed to express their hair, but it makes perfect sense for me. No matter how basic the rest of my presentation is, I feel like it's always there saying something (loudly!) for me.

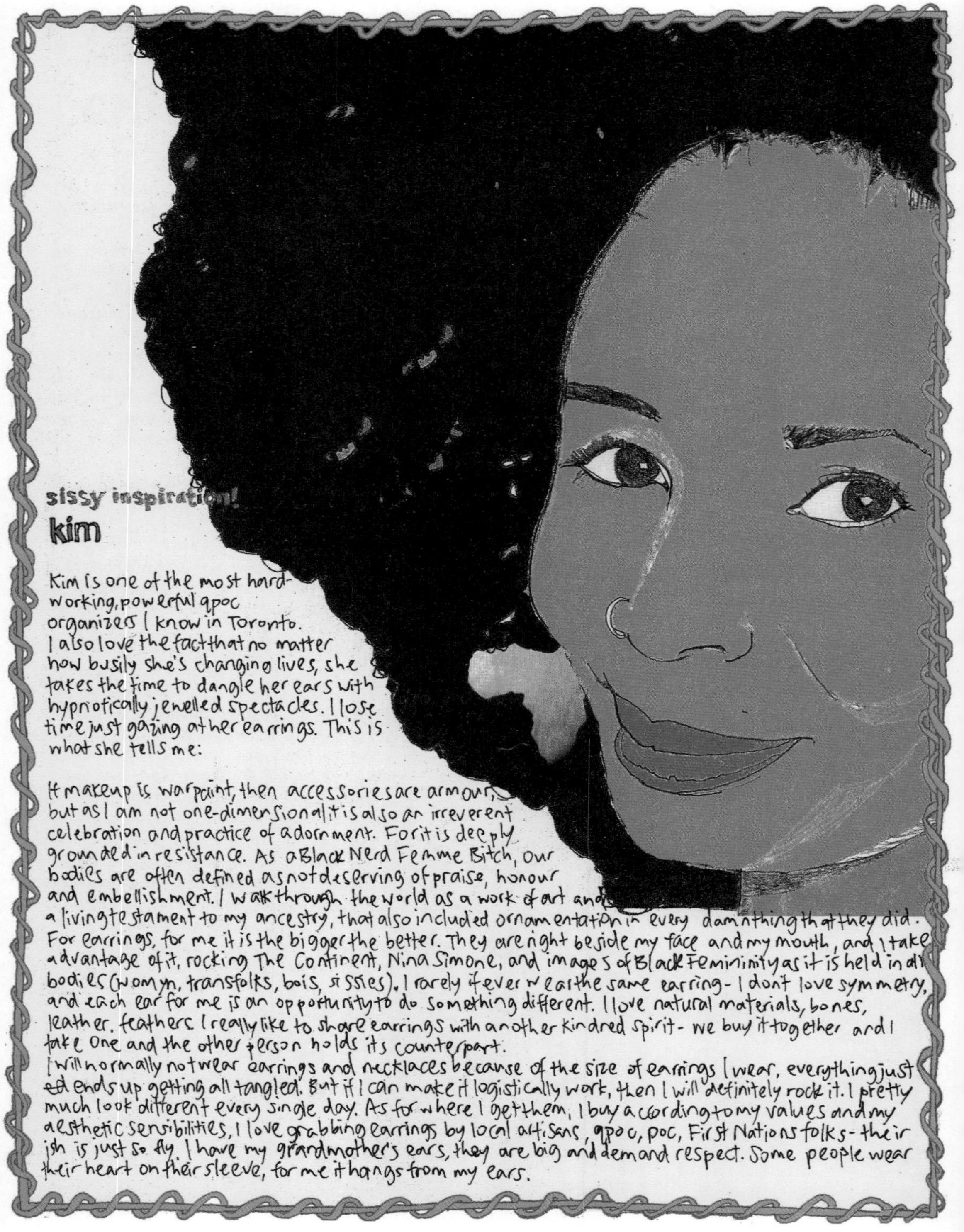

sissy inspiration!

kim

Kim is one of the most hard-working, powerful qpoc organizers I know in Toronto. I also love the fact that no matter how busily she's changing lives, she takes the time to dangle her ears with hypnotically jewelled spectacles. I lose time just gazing at her earrings. This is what she tells me:

If makeup is warpaint, then accessories are armour, but as I am not one-dimensional it is also an irreverent celebration and practice of adornment. For it is deeply grounded in resistance. As a Black Nerd Femme Bitch, our bodies are often defined as not deserving of praise, honour and embellishment. I walk through the world as a work of art and a living testament to my ancestry, that also included ornamentation in every damn thing that they did. For earrings, for me it is the bigger the better. They are right beside my face and my mouth, and I take advantage of it, rocking The Continent, Nina Simone, and images of Black Femininity as it is held in all bodies (womyn, transfolks, bois, sissies). I rarely if ever wear the same earring - I don't love symmetry, and each ear for me is an opportunity to do something different. I love natural materials, bones, leather. feathers I really like to share earrings with another kindred spirit - we buy it together and I take one and the other person holds its counterpart.

I will normally not wear earrings and necklaces because of the size of earrings I wear, everything just ~~ed~~ ends up getting all tangled. But if I can make it logistically work, then I will definitely rock it. I pretty much look different every single day. As for where I get them, I buy acording to my values and my aesthetic sensibilities, I love grabbing earrings by local artisans, qpoc, poc, First Nations folks - their ish is just so fly. I have my grandmother's ears, they are big and demand respect. Some people wear their heart on their sleeve, for me it hangs from my ears.

vivek

In my early twenties, I went through a phase of wearing only oversize athletic wear. One in a series of efforts to not be perceived as weak, pathetic, effeminate. Or in one word: Sissy. A word I heard a lot, a word that made me feel so small. What could be safer than modelling myself after my bullies? I hoped they couldn't see me, hidden under extra fabric and generic sport logos.

Why is the most hurtful word to call someone often associated with femininity?

I didn't realize that every time I winced at the sound of my own voice, every time I concealed my excitement in monotone, every time I believed there was something repulsive about being myself, being a sissy, that I was also perpetuating this misogyny.

Today, I wear my skinny jeans proudly.

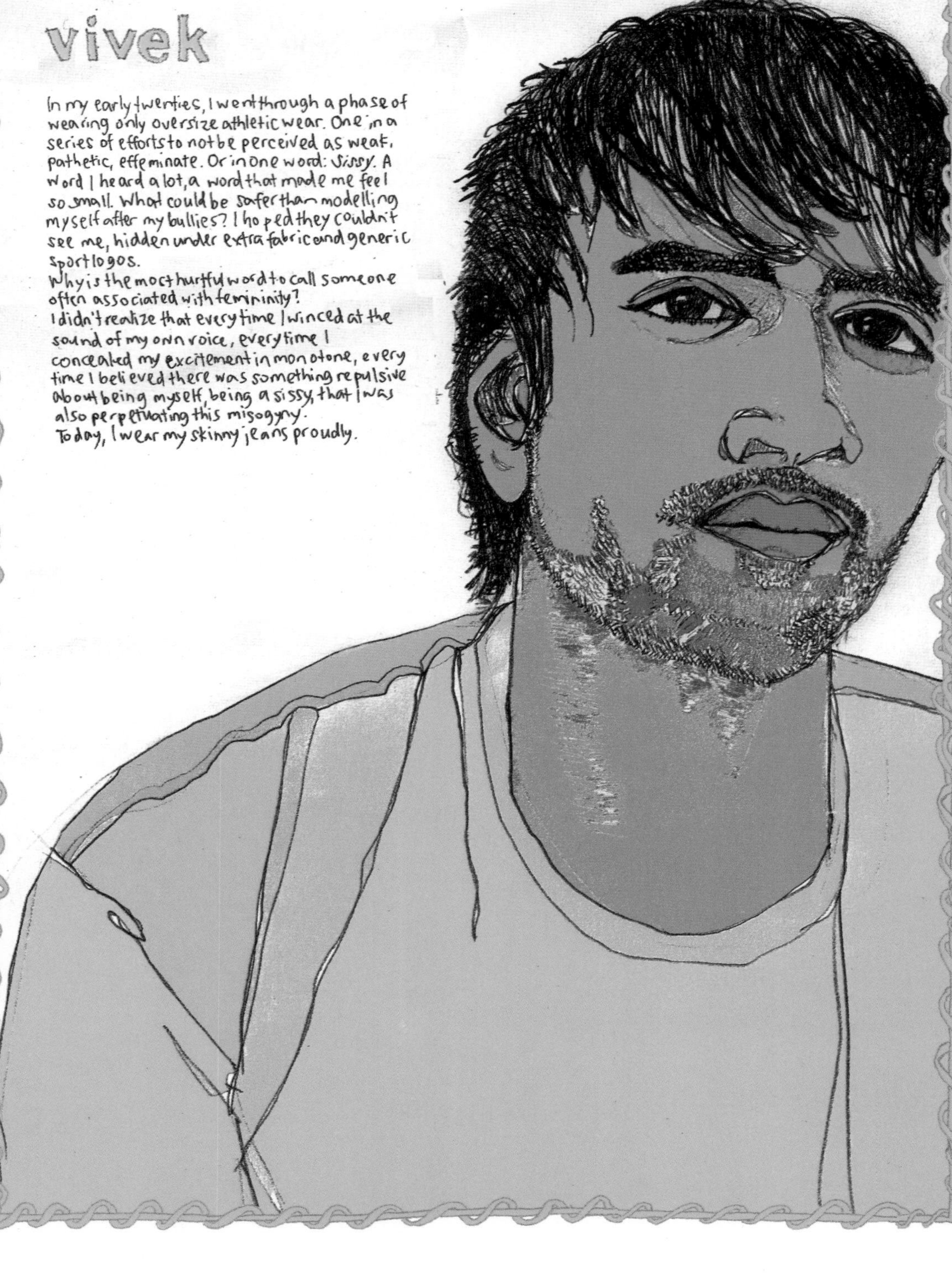

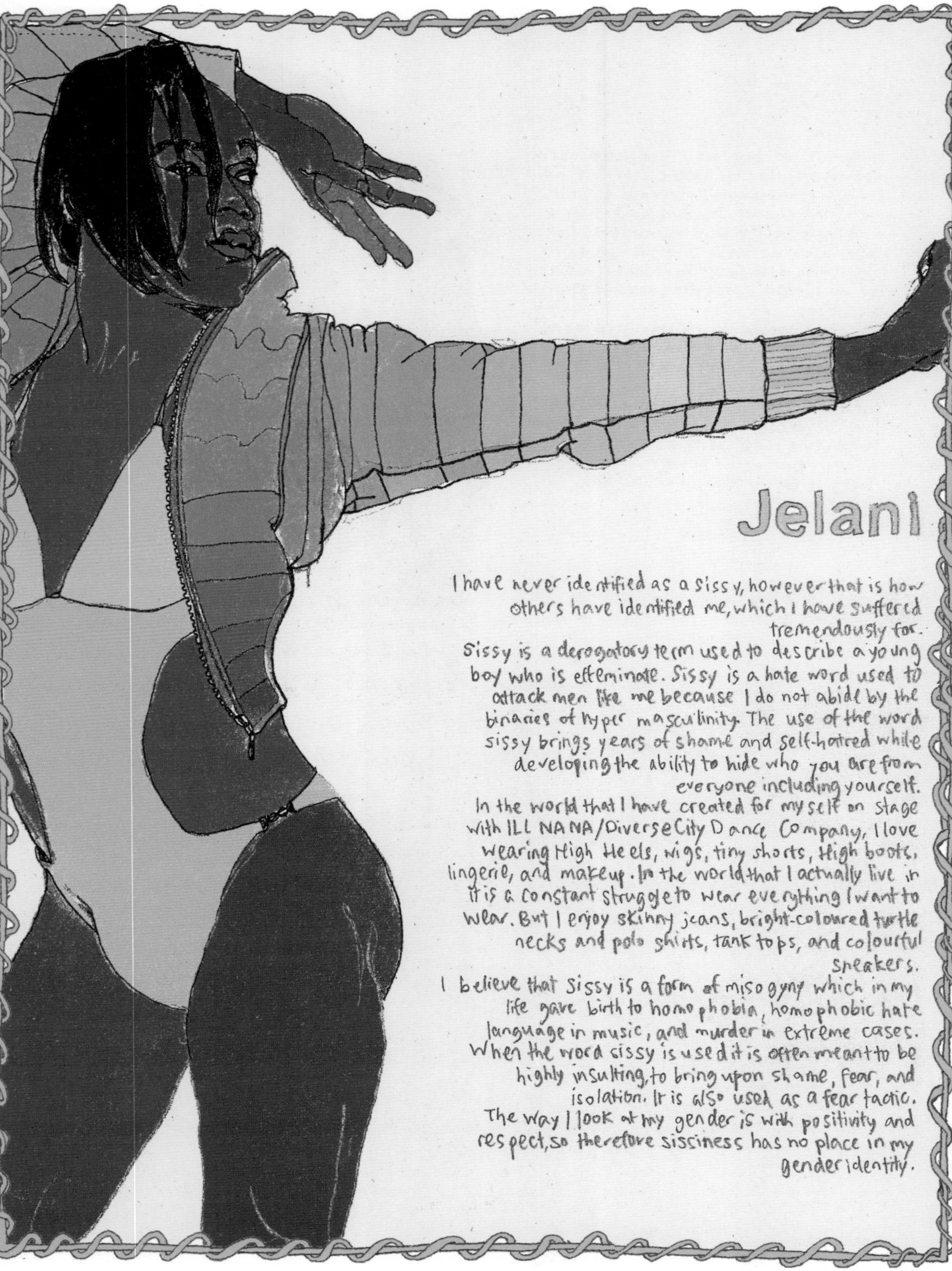

Jelani

I have never identified as a sissy, however that is how others have identified me, which I have suffered tremendously for.

Sissy is a derogatory term used to describe a young boy who is effeminate. Sissy is a hate word used to attack men like me because I do not abide by the binaries of hyper masculinity. The use of the word sissy brings years of shame and self-hatred while developing the ability to hide who you are from everyone including yourself.

In the world that I have created for myself on stage with ILL NANA/DiverseCity Dance Company, I love wearing High Heels, wigs, tiny shorts, High boots, lingerie, and makeup. In the world that I actually live in it is a constant struggle to wear everything I want to wear. But I enjoy skinny jeans, bright-coloured turtle necks and polo shirts, tank tops, and colourful sneakers.

I believe that sissy is a form of misogyny which in my life gave birth to homophobia, homophobic hate language in music, and murder in extreme cases. When the word sissy is used it is often meant to be highly insulting, to bring upon shame, fear, and isolation. It is also used as a fear tactic.

The way I look at my gender is with positivity and respect, so therefore sissiness has no place in my gender identity.

robyn

I'm not shy, and I don't take shit from anybody. That being said though, I'm a mama bear when it comes to my friends. I want to take care of everyone, to cook all us meals as often as possible, and literally tell my nearest 'n' dearest how much I fucking love them every day. A lot of my time is spent doing intensive support and advocacy with people who've been forced into harsh economic, political and social situations by the bullshit rightwing nonsense that our government calls 'liberal democracy', but when I'm with friends (which is often), I'm mostly laughing hysterically about ridiculous things and continuously hugging people, being a total wiener. I would do anything for my people, and am incapable of playing it cool about the overwhelming amount that I feel for them. (I occasionally try but it fails every time). It can take some getting used to, but at this point I'll admit that I am a total gusher/ extreme closet-softie! Shiiit. I did spend a significant percentage of my formative years as a raver though, (and there ain't nothing tough about that), so it's not my fault right? My outfits are 50/50 sissy. Glam-trash for life! My friend Tasha would refer to this as "low-femme." Skid-glamming it up is pretty much my M.O. in a pretty precise balance. Lacey things are so fun, and you can rock that shit with plaid! I would never wear sequins without combat boots, for me it's important to have a wee bit of glam at all times without getting too bougie, know what I mean? I can be serious and extremely hardline about political things that matter to me, but I genuinely believe that we don't need to bring that attitude into our personal lives / it makes people so cold that what's the point of anything?
It is important, useful, and fun as hell to be tough as nails in the outside world, but to me being a sissy can also mean not trying to front and be a cowboy about everything at all times. There can be so much silliness and pressure about how "strong women" are supposed to be somehow macho in all aspects to be taken seriously, but I think we need to remember that sexism also socializes those who are supposed to be "macho" as emotionally stunted much of the time. We all need to embrace our inner sissy as well as our inner tough guy.
It's fine and amazing to be overwhelmed by the beautiful things and people and music that surround us, and to try to front aloofness in the face of all this is futile and a waste of life. I used to feel mildly humiliated about being so damn gushy but I'm slowly coming to terms with it. I want to be able to love hard, rock a mini skirt, and be tough as fuck all at the same time.

sze-yang

I think you grow up to fear your feminine side as if it is all things that make you weak and vulnerable.

Sissy means everything you grow up fearing to be, from childhood into adulthood, encompassing words such as pansy, faggot, flamboyant, girlie, gay. It is often put on the opposite spectrum of what is considered 'good', 'strong', and 'masculine', meaning it is 'bad', 'weak', and 'effeminate' or 'feminine'.

Sissyness is part of my gender identity, though I may not often use the word itself. I think it often refers to feminine energy in reference to men. For me I am very in touch with both sides of myself, both masculine and feminine.

I like to dress as a tomboy aka Aaliyah style, baggie pants, fitted-tight tops, tank tops, and some high tops. I've also been getting into the dangly earrings.

In Super Queeroe ILL NANA/DCDC store, I am a fan of booty shorts, stilettos, on occasion draping fabrics. I grew up often being told I am 'too skinny' and 'weak-looking', as ILL NANA/DCDC I wanted to present an alternative to that notion for myself and others. So since I am in control, I get to be powerful and present my body type out there as something that is both small, strong, and sexy all of the same time! Sissy is something I feared for a long time, and tried to hide, as I became more comfortable with who I am and embraced all sides of me. My sissy gender-bending side is now one of the most powerful sides of myself.

sissy inspiration!

miss vu

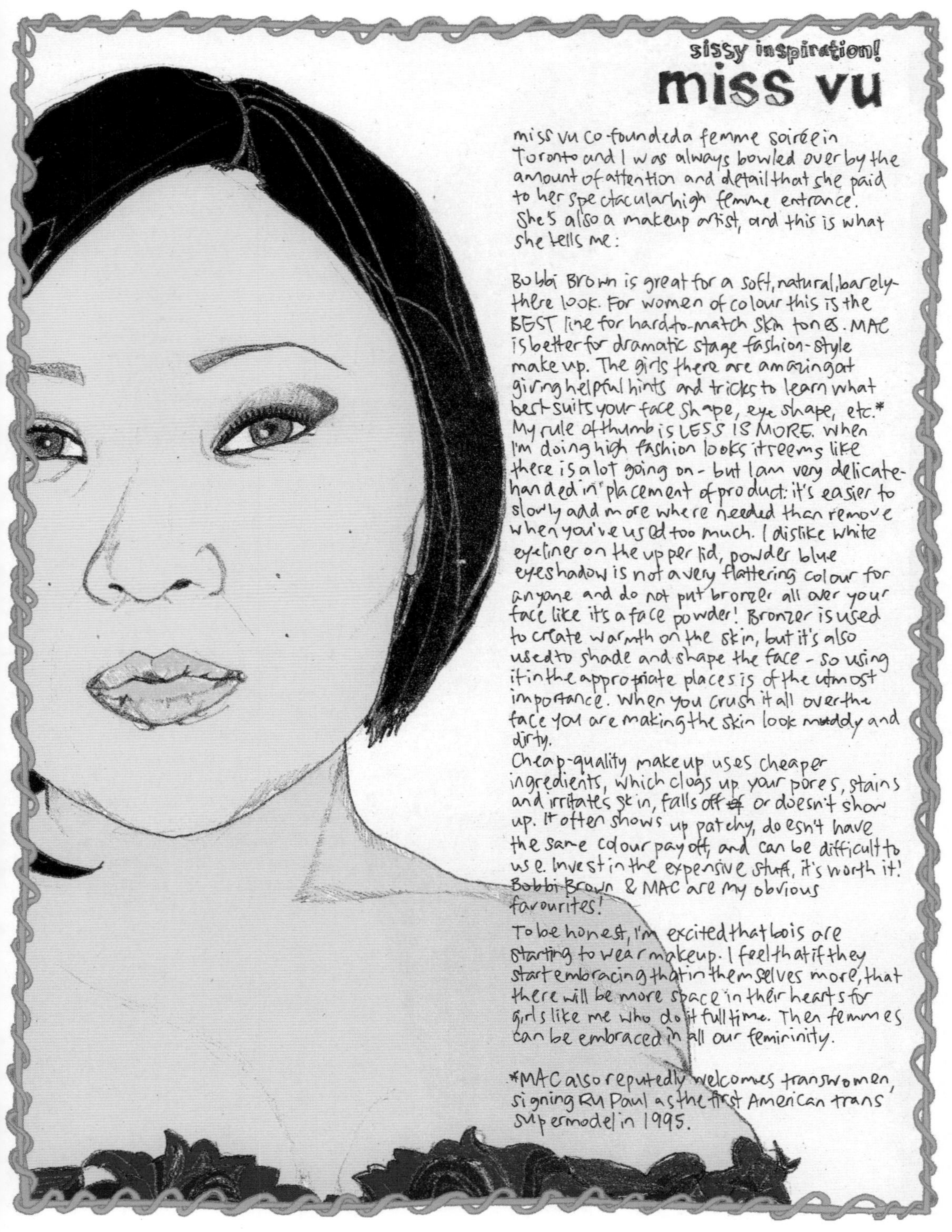

miss vu co-founded a femme soirée in Toronto and I was always bowled over by the amount of attention and detail that she paid to her spectacular high femme entrance. She's also a makeup artist, and this is what she tells me:

Bobbi Brown is great for a soft, natural, barely-there look. For women of colour this is the BEST line for hard-to-match skin tones. MAC is better for dramatic stage fashion-style make up. The girls there are amazing at giving helpful hints and tricks to learn what best suits your face shape, eye shape, etc.* My rule of thumb is LESS IS MORE. When I'm doing high fashion looks it seems like there is a lot going on - but I am very delicate-handed in placement of product: it's easier to slowly add more where needed than remove when you've used too much. I dislike white eyeliner on the upper lid, powder blue eyeshadow is not a very flattering colour for anyone and do not put bronzer all over your face like it's a face powder! Bronzer is used to create warmth on the skin, but it's also used to shade and shape the face - so using it in the appropriate places is of the utmost importance. When you crush it all over the face you are making the skin look muddy and dirty.

Cheap-quality makeup uses cheaper ingredients, which clogs up your pores, stains and irritates skin, falls off ~~of~~ or doesn't show up. It often shows up patchy, doesn't have the same colour payoff, and can be difficult to use. Invest in the expensive stuff, it's worth it! Bobbi Brown & MAC are my obvious favourites!

To be honest, I'm excited that bois are starting to wear makeup. I feel that if they start embracing that in themselves more, that there will be more space in their hearts for girls like me who do it full time. Then femmes can be embraced in all our femininity.

*MAC also reputedly welcomes transwomen, signing RuPaul as the first American trans supermodel in 1995.

raju

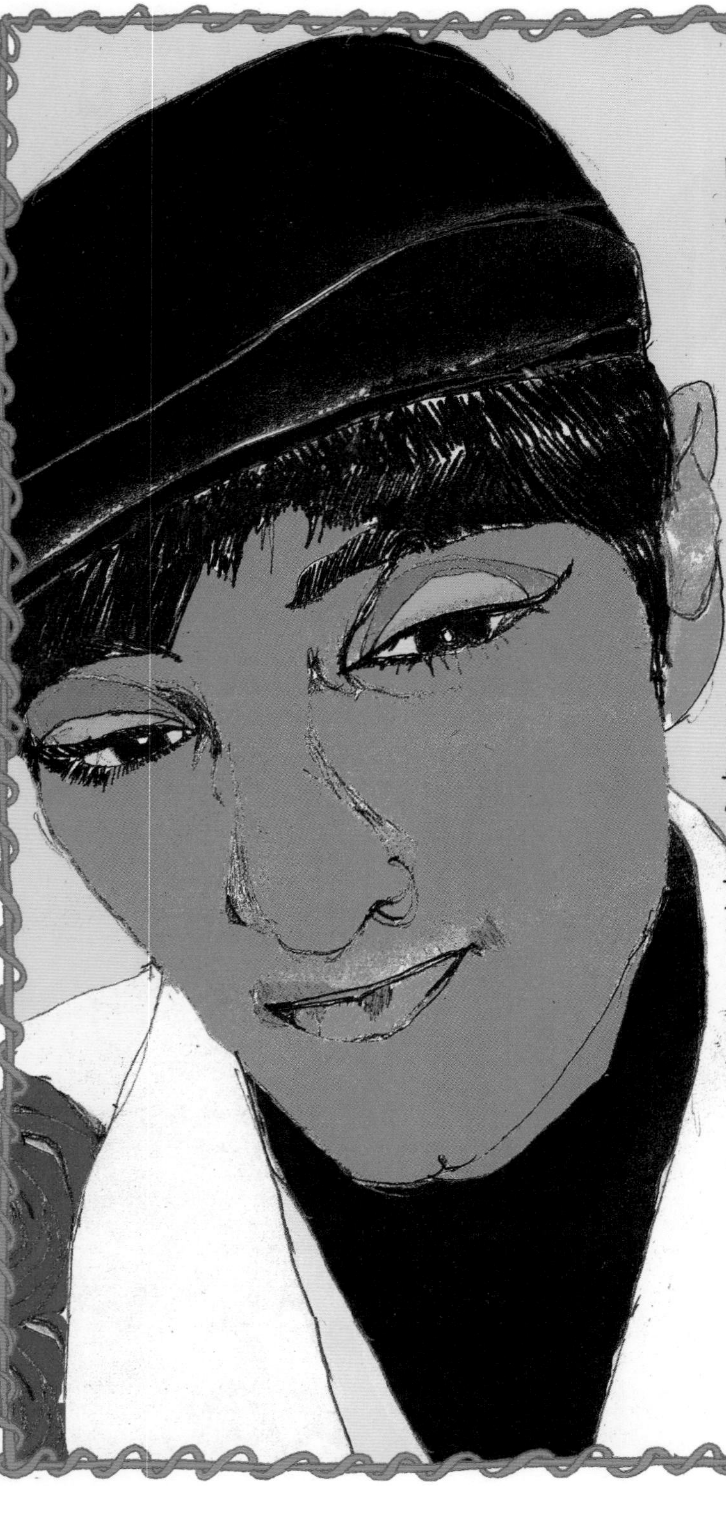

I always thought I hated fashion. Cos it was like you have to measure up, just like with gender, wear the right colour, have the latest style, whatever the hell that was... but then I realized, that's if you're following fashion. I don't like feeling like a sheep and have always been the black one so I said, "I'm just gonna wear what I want." I don't have to follow trends. I can make trends, even if I'm the only one who will follow them. Ha.

So in answer to not fitting in a gender which always required wearing specific clothing in specific ways, I broke the rules: one day I'd wear a leather tie and braces, the next the prettiest, brightest dress. This led from one thing to another. I followed my South Asian roots, basically everything my femme mama taught me, which was to be bold and always coordinate and accessorize. And off I went. At first I was afraid but Lola, my femme alter ego, led the way. She taught me not to be scared of all the haters who would call me a sissy or faggot, not a proper boy or girl, and to embrace my femininity and masculinity on my own terms, and look damn good in the process.

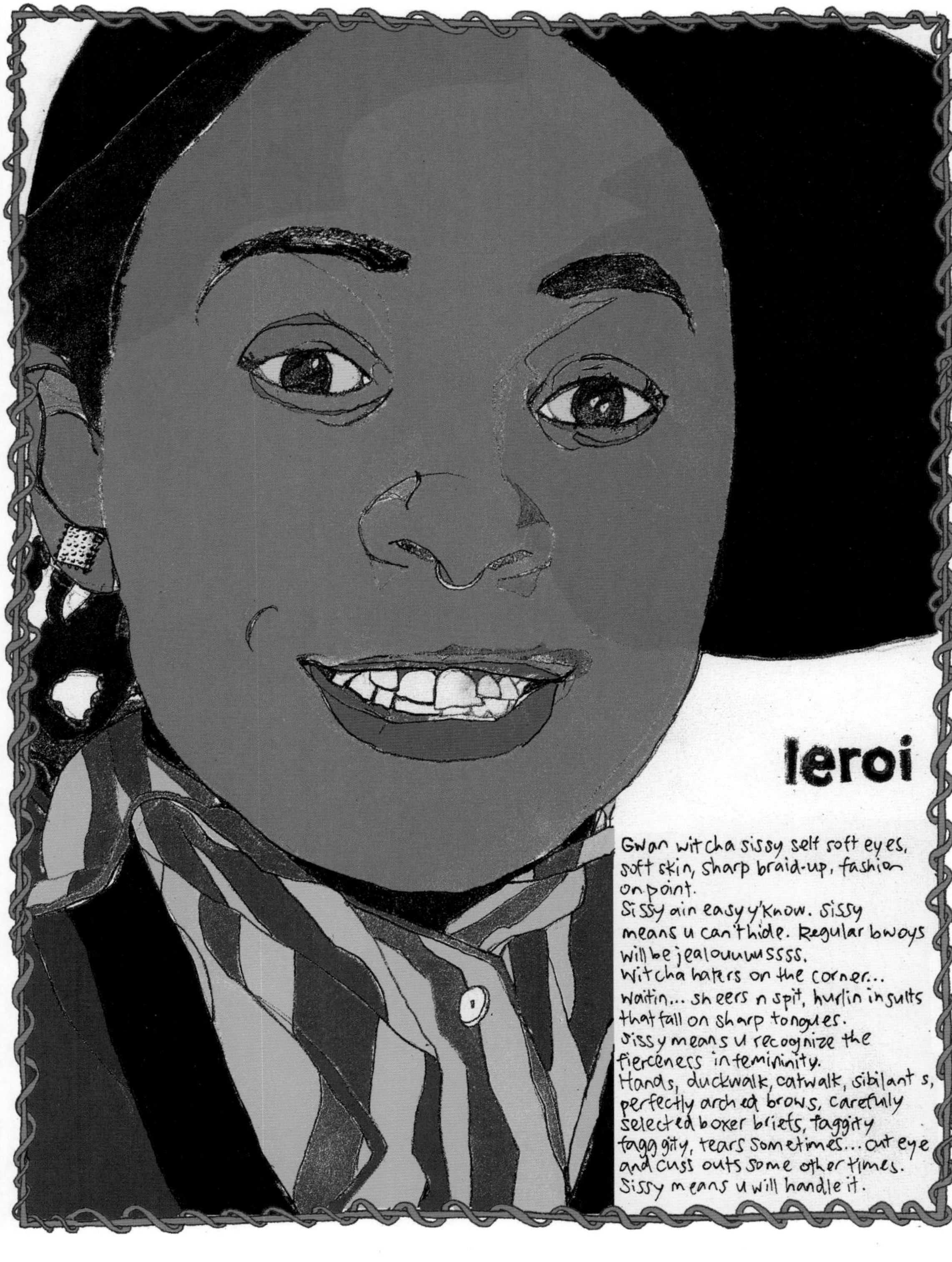
leroi
Gwan witcha sissy self soft eyes,
soft skin, sharp braid-up, fashion
on point.
Sissy ain easy y'know. Sissy
means u can't hide. Regular bwoys
will be jealouuuwussss.
Witcha haters on the corner...
waitin... sneers n spit, hurlin insults
that fall on sharp tongues.
Sissy means u recognize the
fierceness in femininity.
Hands, duckwalk, catwalk, sibilant s,
perfectly arched brows, carefuly
selected boxer briefs, faggity
faggity, tears sometimes... cut eye
and cuss outs some other times.
Sissy means u will handle it.

These are the first two
chapters of a project
called The Hong Moon
Lesbians of the Sacred
Heart. It was first
published in 2012 in the
Sister Spit anthology,
"Writing, Rants &
Reminiscence from the
Road," edited by Michelle
Tea.

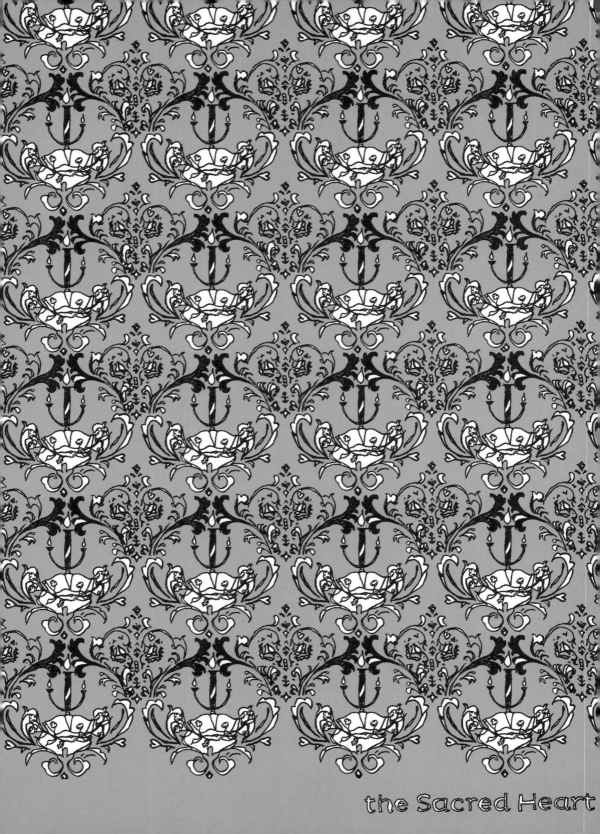

the Sacred Heart

I sort of thought it was normal to be a lesbian because it seemed like we were all lesbians at our Singaporean secondary school.

It could be because it was a catholic convent girls' school, which seem to have a pattern of producing lesbians. Or it could be because of Ling Ling, who was the coolest girl in our school, and as queer as the sisters were pious.

But her coolness wasn't as much about who she was, as it was about what she was: an American. That made her completely magnetic. You could even argue that some of us were lesbians indirectly because of the command of the American empire.

While I realize I could face some opinions to the contrary, especially from the school staff, these are, to the best of my recollection, my own true and factual memoirs of growing up as one of the many lesbians of the Convent of the Sacred Heart.

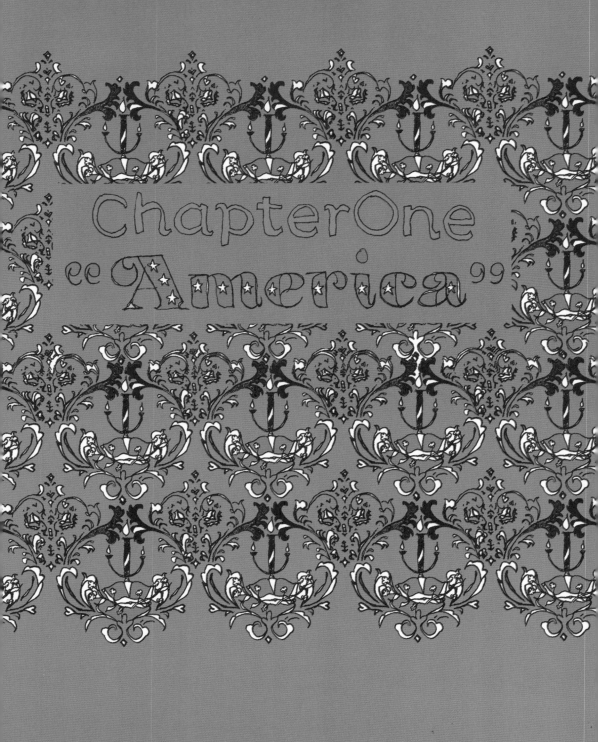

ChapterOne
"America"

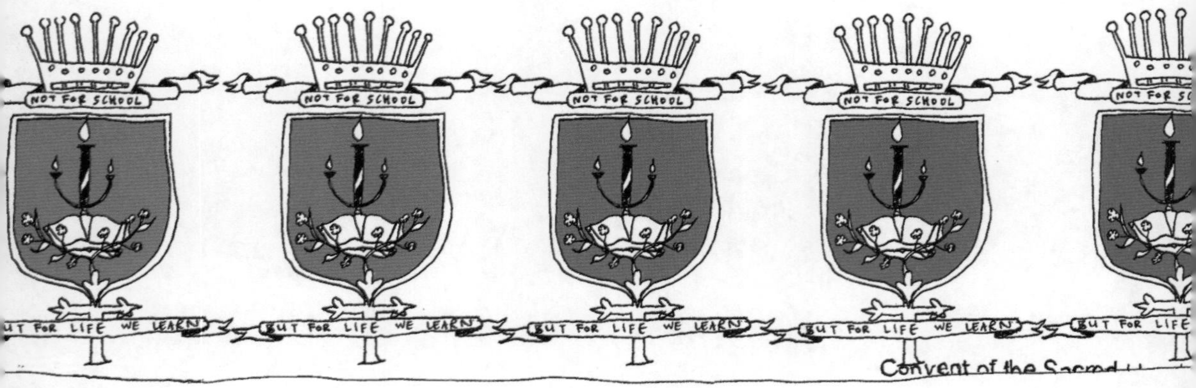
NOT FOR SCHOOL
BUT FOR LIFE WE LEARN
Convent of the

There are six billion of us in the world who do not come from North America, and we know what it's like to live in its shadow – to grow up hearing, seeing, reading, watching, discussing, interpreting and obsessing over it.

But it's like sex. Until you really get to know it, your idea is inaccurate and exaggerated. Just as Americans have absurd exotic notions of any other country, we have absurd exotic notions about America. Except that unlike the single ignorant, misconceived notion America has about our country, we have infinite ignorant, misconceived notions about it.

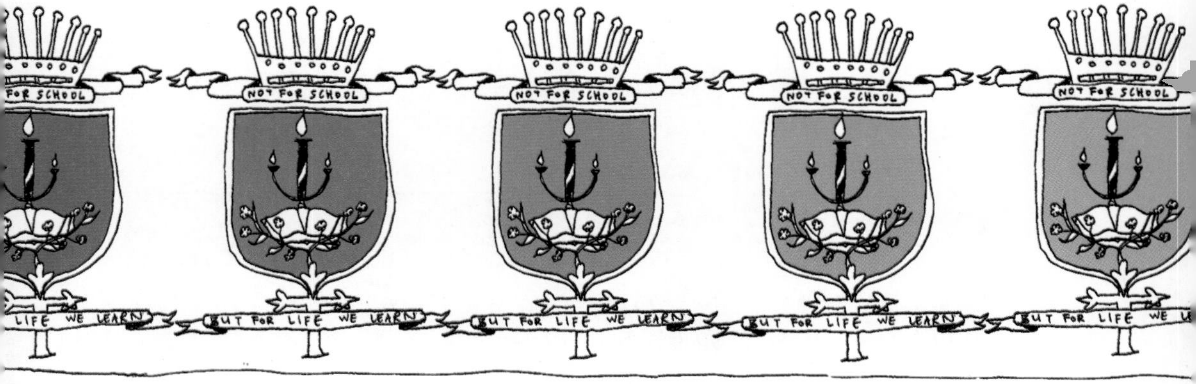
NOT FOR SCHOOL
BUT FOR LIFE WE LEARN

And we have to entertain them all, because like sex, no matter what you think of it, you can't even try to escape it. You can't be disinterested or decide to ignore it. If you did, you would have to take up a radical alternative lifestyle like religious service. It's indisputably powerful, and it pervades, influences and controls your life in an insidious way. You might chase it, imitate it, condemn or even fight it, but you can't get rid of it.

"But wait," you might say. "I don't want to hear about America. I want to hear about the LESBIANS."
Yes, that's true. But in order to explain the culture of my Singaporean school and the influence of trendsetters like Ling Ling, I have to explain the idea of "America." And I don't mean real life everyday nine-to-five America, but I mean the shiny, inflated, successfully exported branding of the Leader of the Free World.

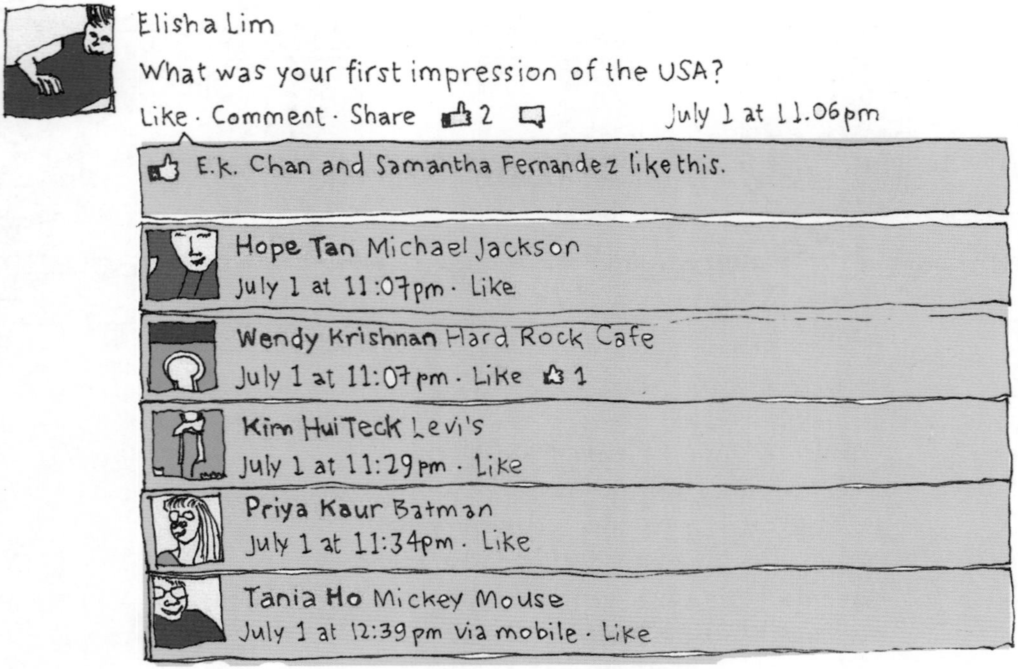
Elisha Lim
What was your first impression of the USA?
Like · Comment · Share 2
July 1 at 11.06pm
E.K. Chan and Samantha Fernandez like this.
Hope Tan Michael Jackson
July 1 at 11:07pm · Like
Wendy Krishnan Hard Rock Cafe
July 1 at 11:07pm · Like 1
Kim Hui Teck Levi's
July 1 at 11:29pm · Like
Priya Kaur Batman
July 1 at 11:34pm · Like
Tania Ho Mickey Mouse
July 1 at 12:39pm via mobile · Like

The King of Pop, Michael Jackson, was an American. He had his own golden statue, Coca-Cola commercials, the moonwalk and the high-tech head-blending technology of the 1991 music video for "Black or White."

Hard Rock Cafe was excellent American PR. It reinforced the Legendary Status of American and British music and the Sacred Value of All of its Debris. It established American mythology and legend, as well as exorbitantly priced exotic dishes like Poppers, Buffalo Wings, Jacket Potatoes, and New York Cheesecake.

Levi's is how Americans looked. The posters featured impossibly tall, rosy-cheeked models who looked dashing and sophisticated in flannel shirts. We dutifully donned these in our suffocatingly humid climate.

Despite its subversive anti-hero, Batman was one of the many movies that promoted American superiority. Gotham city, based on New York, had its own magnificent vigilante who sacrificed everything to protect his beloved city. He also boasted a wealthy high-status lineage, a beautiful white girlfriend and even a servile English butler.

Mickey Mouse was clean, plastic, flawless, tacky, expensive, clichéd, mass-produced, and totally ubiquitous.

Beverly Hills 90210 exported the rules of American decorum. It was important to make pointed, cynical assertions and to be sarcastic. It was often necessary to humble other people. It was important to be popular.
* Popular didn't mean friendly and well-liked. It meant that your appearance, finances and sex life were superior to everyone else's.

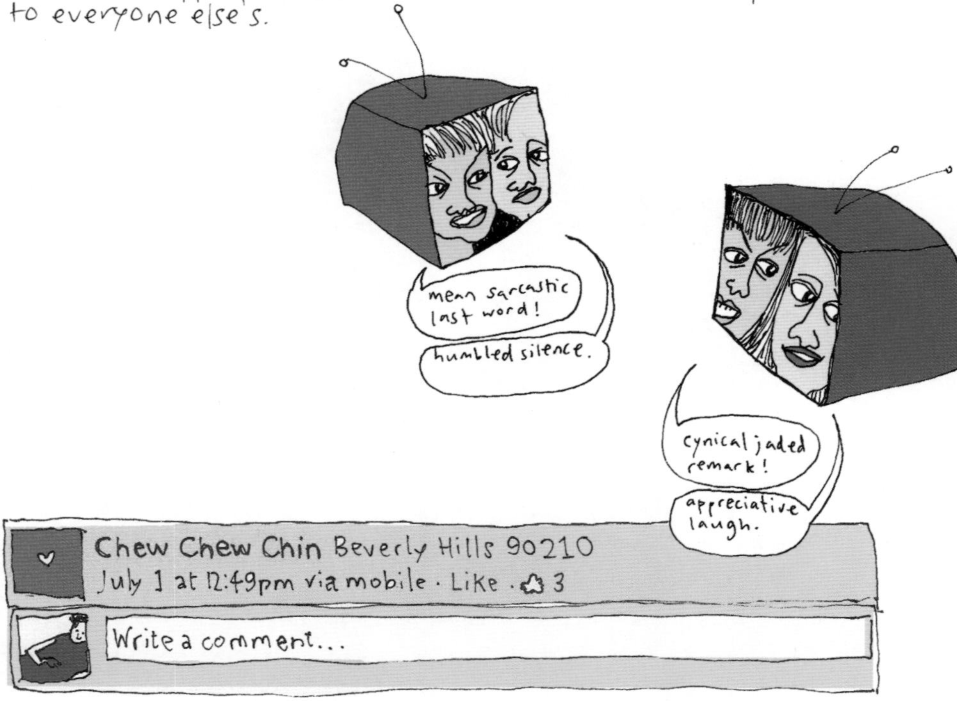
mean sarcastic last word!
humbled silence.
cynical jaded remark!
appreciative laugh.
Chew Chew Chin Beverly Hills 90210
July 1 at 12:49pm via mobile · Like · 3
Write a comment...

Chapter Two

Ling Ling

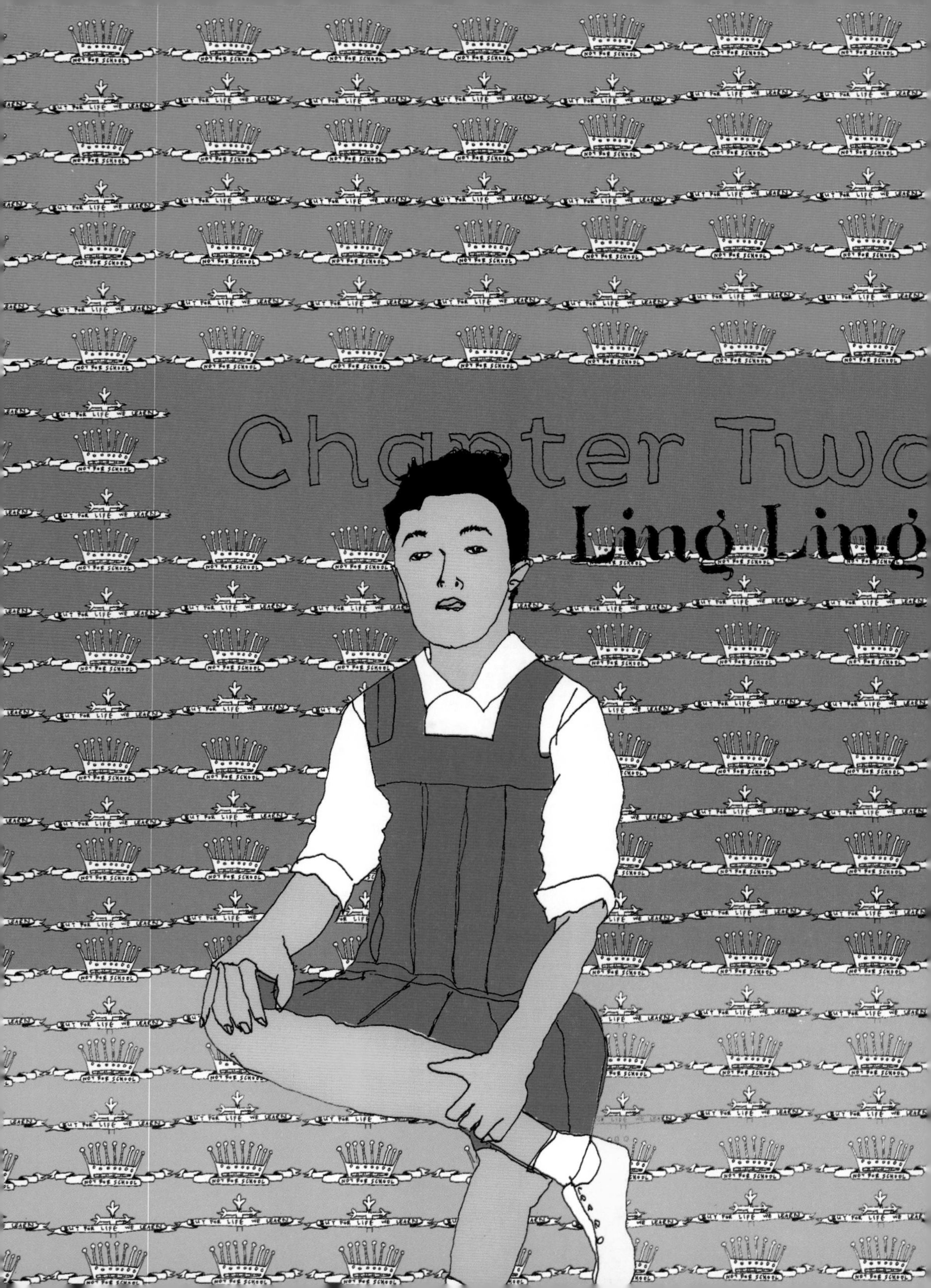
NOT FOR SCHOOL
BUT FOR LIFE WE LEARN

At the Convent of the Sacred Heart, Ling Ling was our resident American. She wasn't even American at all, she was said to have spent one year in Pennsylvania when she was eight years old. But it had been enough to teach her the American accent. Matched with her relentless charisma, she was all-powerful.

The Name

Ling Ling's last name was Han, which if you pronounce traditionally, rhymes with "fawn." But Ling Ling preferred to preserve the pronunciation she had been assigned in the States, which was a hopelessly mispronounced Han that rhymed with "fan," but in a really long lazy "fayn."

This might not seem like much of a difference, but no one ever opened up their vowels that wide. Even just the struggle of executing the sound could turn heads in the hallway.

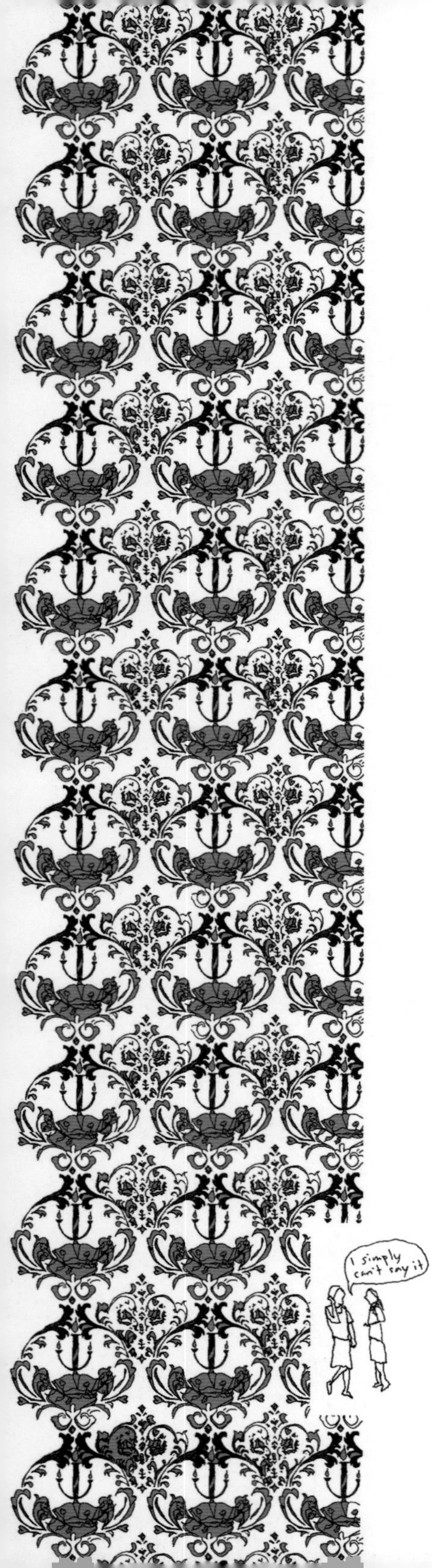
I simply can't say it

The Music

On special occasions, each class could take turns performing a dance routine in front of the whole school. Some classes did local traditional dances and some did interpretations of popular radio songs. Ling Ling kind of made history by dancing to songs that we had never heard of. They came from America and they were called hip hop.

This was something that never played on our radio stations. Our only Western station played America's Top Forty songs that only got as racy as Duran Duran.

Ling Ling's dance number shook with the most seductive, provocative rhythm and bass lines our convent stage had ever exhibited. It wasn't that we became immediately intoxicated with hip hop, because it didn't have any context in our lives. We were mainly in awe of its messenger.

Was Ling Ling a good dancer? Now I can't even remember. I just remember that we worked ourselves into a feverish swoon while she gyrated in front of her backup dancers and pushed it, pushed it good.

highly coordinated backup dancers
<......

no belt!
totally against
the rules...

Recess

Ling Ling played basketball and
that's just clearly sexy. But she
took it to another level
because nobody played
basketball. We had been
colonized by England, not
America, and so we had
inherited netball, which is a
very graceful nimble sport
where the ball flies quickly
through the air and never
touches the ground.

But basketball players dribble.
So when Ling Ling hit the court
there was suddenly the sound
of a ball furiously smacking
cement, pumping under skirts,
flexing between tanned legs
and other lewd macho acts. No
one knew what America was
like, but we imagined that Ling
Ling's basketball court was a
little American theatre.

The Walk

Ling Ling had also picked up some kind of enigmatic body language while she was in America. She had a swagger that no one else could pull off. She swayed through the halls like she had a ten-pound gun holster on each hip.

It might have been the power strut of any neighbourhood gangster, but when she matched it with her exaggerated American jowly vowels, it felt just like a visit from Brandon Walsh from the television series Beverly Hills 90210.

Disclosure

Okay, so it's time to confess
that I was an American, too.

There didn't seem to be a point
in admitting it before now.
After all, I wasn't the kind of
American that Ling Ling was.
I didn't have the same power. I
was more docile, obedient and
conformist. The trouble was I
was a Canadian.

I'd moved from Canada to
Singapore when I was ten, and
by the time I'd reached
secondary school, it was clear
that I was foreign. I was bigger
somehow. I could be louder and
funnier and more easily noticed.
I sometimes hoped that I could
use this to attract Ling Ling's
attention. On the rare occasion
that I was in her presence, I'd
try to draw out my accent to
be more like her, really forcing
the letter 'r' and snorting a lot.

But I just didn't seem to
understand Singaporean culture
enough to harness the same
kind of awe that she did.
I think you'd have to be local to
do that.

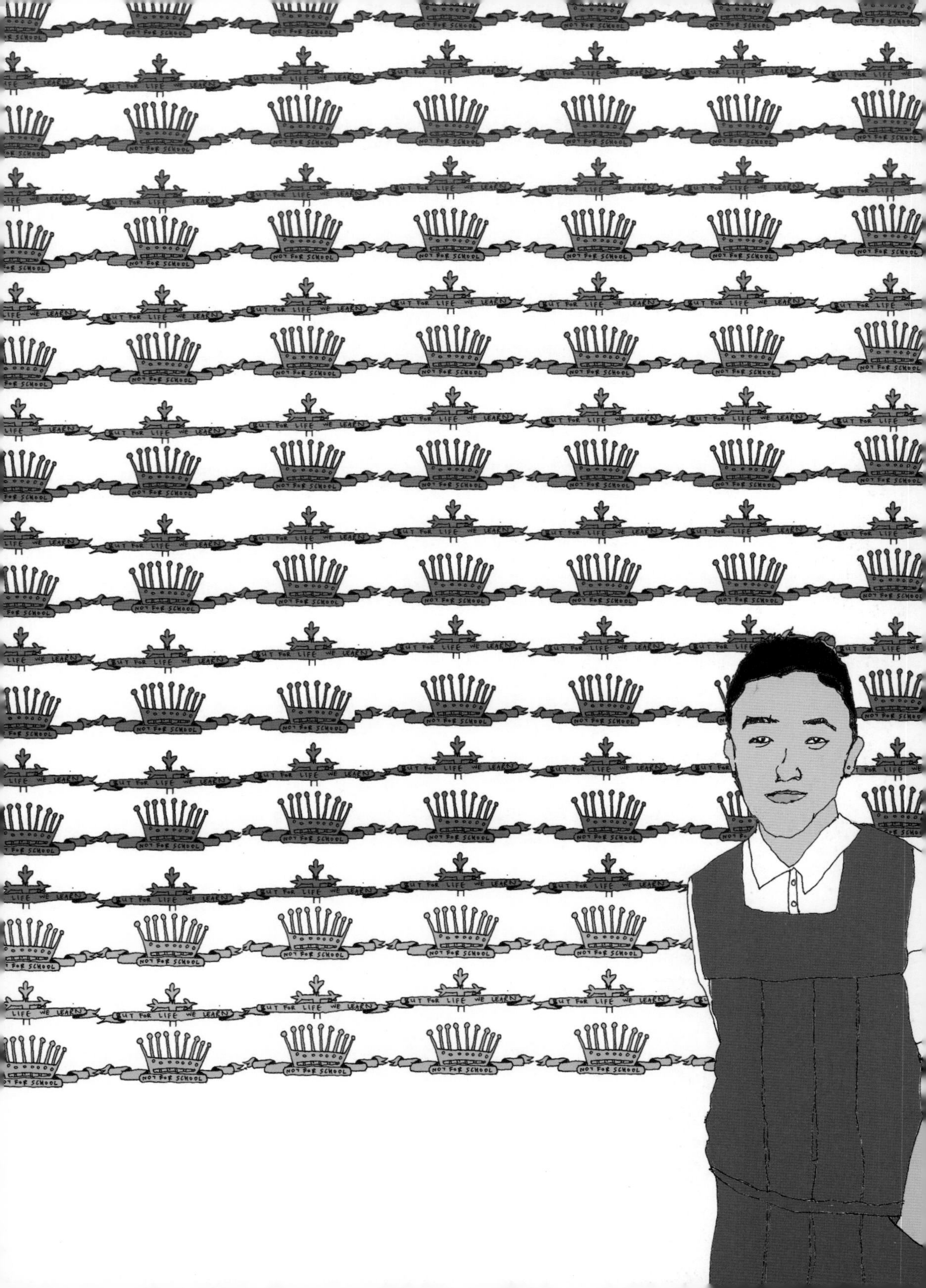
NOT FOR SCHOOL
BUT FOR LIFE WE LEARN

One of my favourite
queer projects has been
our bold collective
experiment with the
pronoun "They."
The interview with Rae
was first published in the
queer art magazine No
More Potlucks, Jan/Feb
2012.

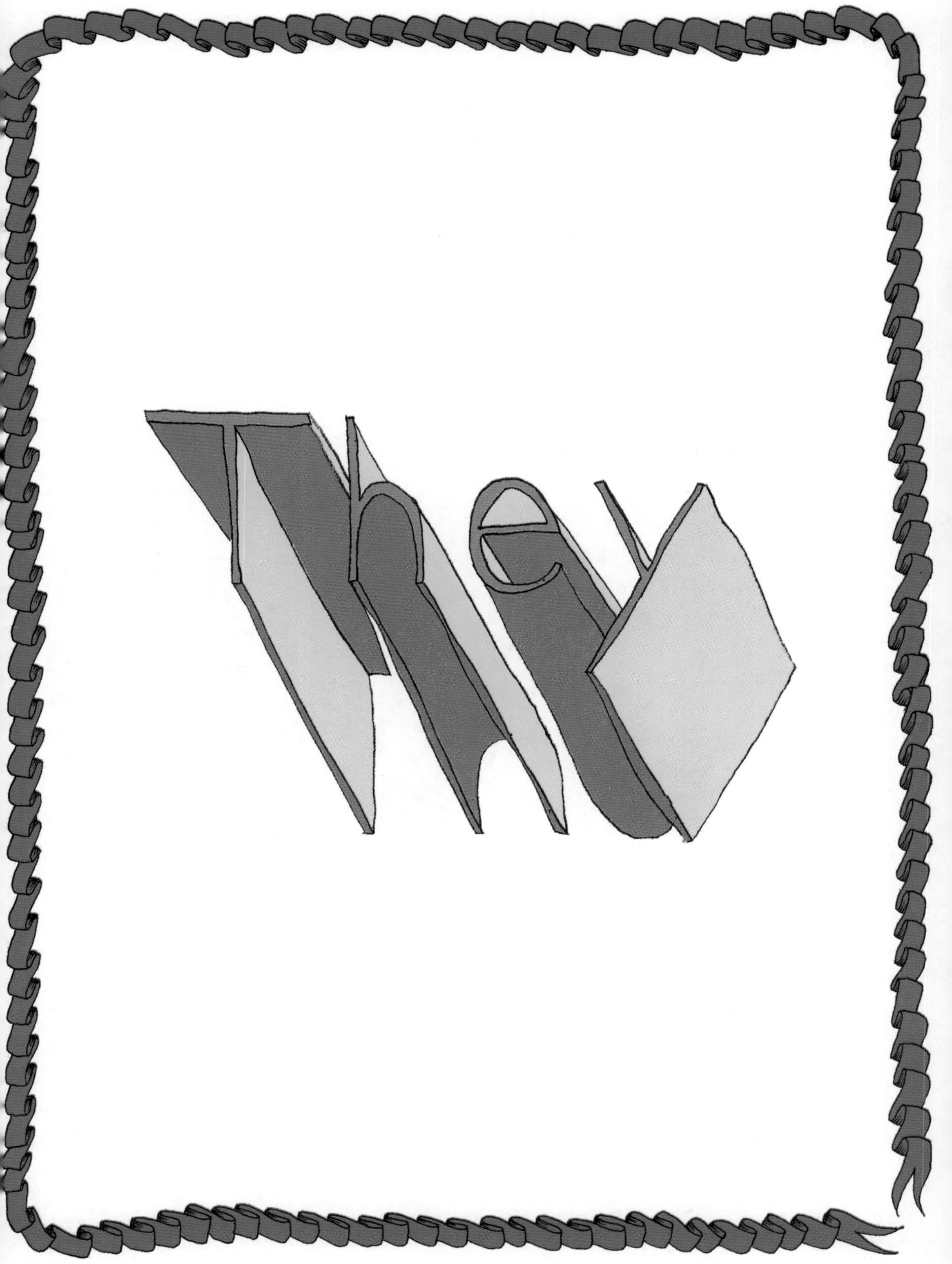
They

Hari was the first person I knew to use the pronoun "they." We were roommates, and I confronted them on their bed. "What's going on?" I said. "You were my last fellow butch in town!"

I was not supportive. I was threatened, and a bit envious. Very envious, I guess, which is why I was mad. I started off reluctantly practicing Hari's pronoun, carefully and awkwardly, and then one day I noticed with amazement that gender had dropped out of the bottom of my idea of Hari altogether. Someone called them 'she' by mistake, and not only did it sound wrong, it sounded weird. My roommate isn't a 'he' or a 'she,' I realized, they're a floating in-between gender invention. It had worked. And so, gingerly, sheepishly, and gratefully, I realized that I could do it too.

Hari quit the gender binary and it wasn't that trendy at the time, and there wasn't a lot of enthusiasm or support for it. It was their own tough decision to jump off the track and walk away, towards freedom. Which is lucky for me, who got to follow.

Hari Eshmanan

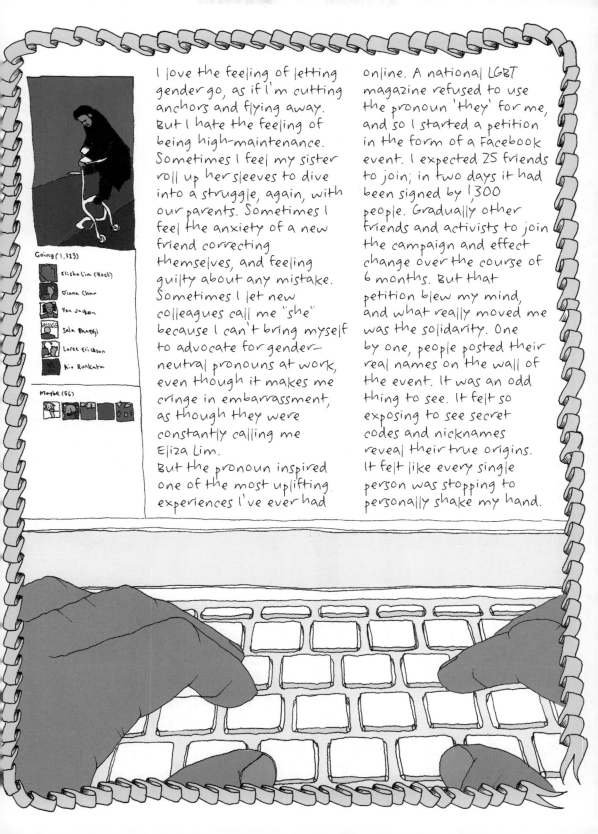

I love the feeling of letting gender go, as if I'm cutting anchors and flying away. But I hate the feeling of being high-maintenance. Sometimes I feel my sister roll up her sleeves to dive into a struggle, again, with our parents. Sometimes I feel the anxiety of a new friend correcting themselves, and feeling guilty about any mistake. Sometimes I let new colleagues call me "she" because I can't bring myself to advocate for gender-neutral pronouns at work, even though it makes me cringe in embarrassment, as though they were constantly calling me Eliza Lim.

But the pronoun inspired one of the most uplifting experiences I've ever had online. A national LGBT magazine refused to use the pronoun 'they' for me, and so I started a petition in the form of a Facebook event. I expected 25 friends to join; in two days it had been signed by 1,300 people. Gradually other friends and activists to join the campaign and effect change over the course of 6 months. But that petition blew my mind, and what really moved me was the solidarity. One by one, people posted their real names on the wall of the event. It was an odd thing to see. It felt so exposing to see secret codes and nicknames reveal their true origins. It felt like every single person was stopping to personally shake my hand.

Going (1,313)

Elisha Lim (Host)
Diana Chan
Yen Jackson
Sala Bhadaji
Loree Erickson
Kio Runkata

Maybe (56)

Elisha: So Rae, how do you find those little inroads where a mainstream crowd actually feels safe enough to support you? Like where I can say, "I'm never gonna draw another white person again" and white people applaud? How do you manage to criticize transphobia in front of a hipster audience and have them love it?

Rae: It's as long as everybody feels like they're "in the club." If you said, 'hey, all of you are racist,' and in fact they all are, I mean we all are, it wouldn't have the same effect. That's the beauty of art. It takes you places you wouldn't go. Sometimes I invite them into the queer world. Sometimes people want to be invited, you know. You just have to find the way to perform it. Get a publicist. Get someone to promote you in magazines and on the radio. You need to get a presence. There's nothing wrong with that, just making some money. I mean, I want a nice life.

Elisha: Hah, yeah. So what's a nice life?

Rae: You know, not thinking about being trans all the time. To have a home. A group of people that use my pronoun right.

Elisha: That's tragic.

Rae: Hahahahah... a nice life is when people get my pronoun right.

Actually, I've been looking for a chance to come out as 'they' and maybe this is it. I'm going by 'they' now. I'm gender-retired. I'm no good at gender.

Elisha: Let's high five to 'they!'

Rae: Yeah. Rae Spoon is using 'they.' I mean, it helped me to see your petition.

Elisha: No way! Oh my god, that is amazing! It was an amazing petition with 1,500 people signing up to force a gay paper to call me 'they.' But I felt like I let the ball drop. I never got them to do it.

Rae: But that helped me to say, yeah, now it's time. I got permission from you to use 'they' and I could see people supporting it.

Elisha: Oh my god, that's incredibly heartening....

Stand By Your Trans- a duet by Elisha Lim and Rae Spoon

Rae Spoon

Kit and I drove across Ontario telling stories about being transfolks of colour. I had schemed to make art and money and freedom, but in the end my favourite part was spending every weekend with someone wonderful. This is how Kit talks about gender.

"I started using 'they' because it was a perfect way to name a gender that I couldn't name; it was beside, beyond and within all the ways I saw gender expressed around me. I needed a way for people to know that I was changing, fluid, and Not A Boy. I needed people to recognize my dynamic gender, so that I could be Recognized. But then I stopped.

"Now I go by 'she.' Male is viewed as neutral in western patriarchy, and when folks are assigned male at birth but don't want to be 'men' but 'in-between,' their expressions of gender weirdness often get read as 'male.' In my experience, when people think 'androgynous,' they think about someone who acts masculine even though they are female-assigned. When I was looking at the people around me who were genderqueer, I wasn't seeing myself.

"For me, for better or for worse, transition is in part about recognition. Using 'they' meant that people still saw me as a boy. I wasn't associated with genderqueer because I was/am easily gendered male, and in the end it was not enough of the recognition that I wanted or needed.

"The notion of defining, naming and flagging is powerful, but also creates ideas of what something has to be in order to be that thing. I wasn't fitting the idea of what expressions of 'genderqueer' were. And I, frankly, deal with enough isolation.

"I find huge inspiration in the trans women I've met. I found more alliance and relatable stories in the experiences of trans women with more masculine identities. There is an amazing history of trans women breaking down gender and I want people to know that those actions lead to people like me.

"It doesn't mean I've become a rigid essentialist focussed on a binary. It means I found a place I belong. And like everything, that might change. I'm all about transitions."

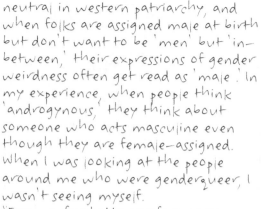

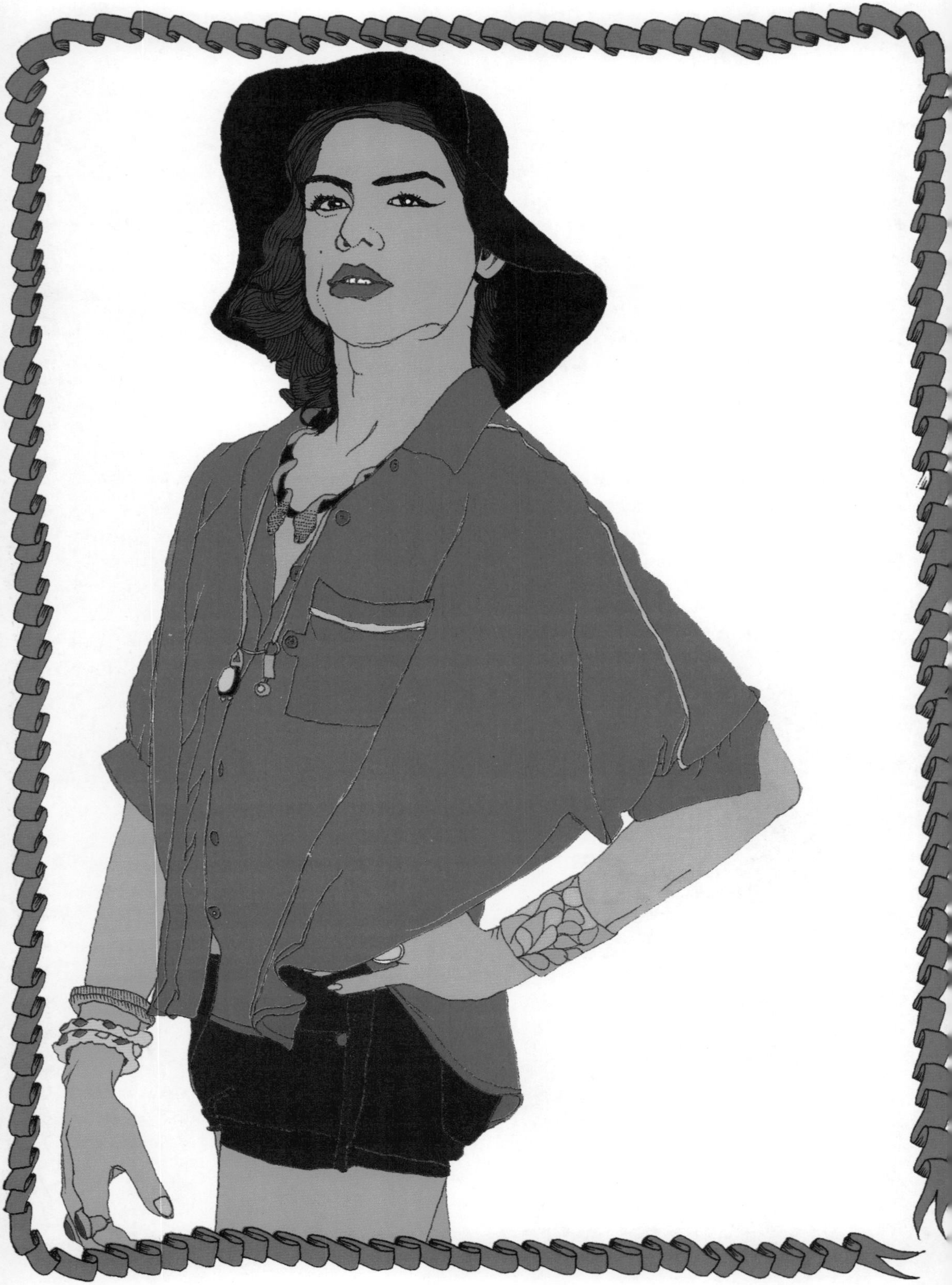

Kiley May

It's so hard not to love Kiley May. When I first saw them on a panel about race and gender, I felt a little suspicious. Who is this stranger, speaking like a new queer authority out of the blue? But before they were finished, I was looking for excuses to go up and say hi. They were so frank and genuine that I trusted them completely. This is what they have to say.

"For this photo shoot I did my makeup and lipstick in front of my mum for the first time. It was a big deal for me, considering I used to hide myself from her.

"Using gender-neutral pronouns feels most correct and appropriate for my self and my body, because my gender identity feels neutral. I am Mohawk, I am Kanie'keha:ka and Hotinonshon:ni. In the colonial English language, I identify as Two-Spirit.

"Basically, I don't fully feel like a woman and I definitely don't feel like a man. I feel like a gender hybrid, a mix between female and male. My gender identity is its own special category. Being called 'he' makes me feels gross, it does not match how I feel inside. The same with being called 'she.' Though it's better than 'he,' it still feels incorrect. I really like 'they, their, them' pronouns because it addresses and acknowledges my female and male energies, and it feels like a much better fit than binary pronouns. When someone refers to me as 'they,' it just feels so right and so good.

"The fact that my mum took these photos is a reflection of how far we have come, and how much she accepts me and celebrates me. She was totally directing me to pose more femme, flip my hair back, open up my shirt, give more sass to the camera.

"When we finished I hugged her and told her how much it meant for me, that it was a big moment of validation and acceptance from her. And she said, 'You have so much beauty to share with the world.'

"I feel really fortunate, lucky and blessed to have my mother and family."

jealousy

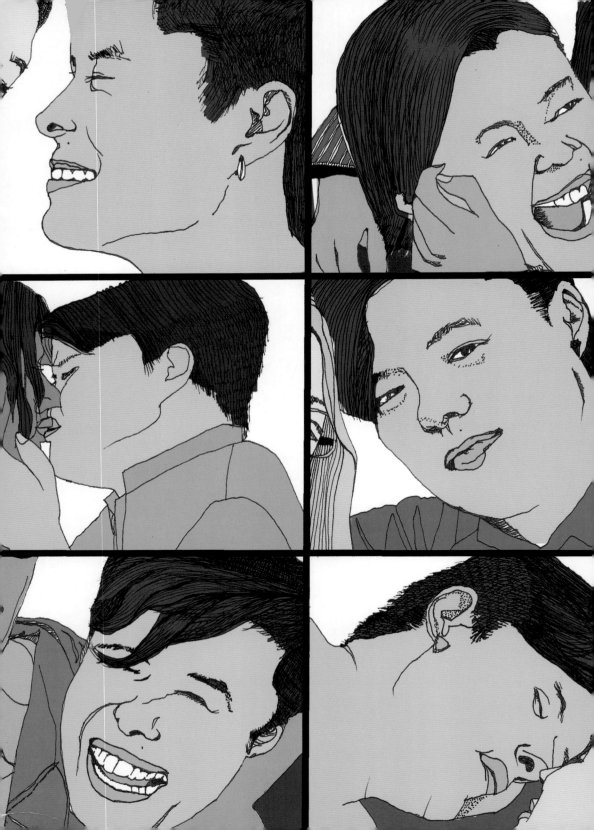

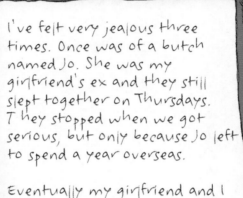

I've felt very jealous three times. Once was of a butch named Jo. She was my girlfriend's ex and they still slept together on Thursdays. They stopped when we got serious, but only because Jo left to spend a year overseas.

Eventually my girlfriend and I became monogamous, but she said that when Jo came back, the Thursday sleepovers would resume.

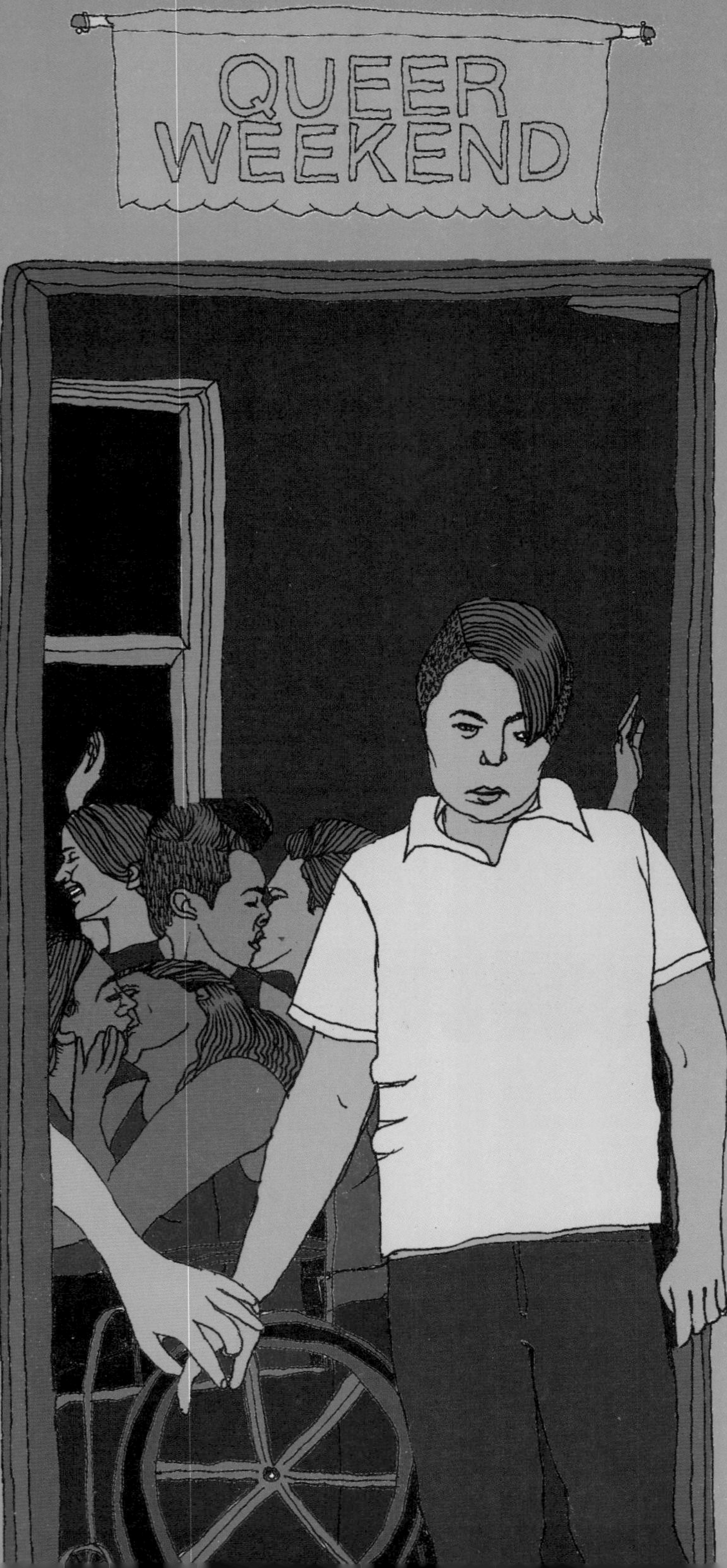
QUEER WEEKEND

Jealousy sank like claws into my gut, deeper than she could probably ever realize. I panicked with a terror that felt older than my ability to love.

I started to play mental reruns of Jo. I had only seen her once at a Queer Weekend. She'd had an attractive queer in her lap laughing uproariously at her joke. My picture of her was cultured, assiduous and brilliant. She was probably an asset to her graduate department. She had gone overseas for some kind of residency. She might have been an artist or a writer. She was probably working on an indispensable contribution to the literary canon.

She grew mightier in my head all year. It felt like I was down a hole I couldn't climb out of. I fought with my girlfriend. I told her that she should stop sleeping with Jo. She told me that I was bringing out her worst.

Jo eventually came back. I never saw her, I just saw my girlfriend walk out the door one Thursday afternoon and not return until Sunday. It was near the end of our relationship.

Frien

Q

7pm

Thu

Thu
2 new

Wed

Tue

Mon

Sun

Sat

Fri

Fri

Fri

Eng
Mor

Elisha Lim   3:02pm

My next girlfriend had an important ex, and they were
still close, too. The ex's name was Ri Luo, and they would
write long-distance emails to each other that I assumed
were profound and erotic.

Ri Luo was a disabled artist and the life of the party. I
pictured her as a charming hostess clinking a wine glass at
dinner in siren red lipstick, a pretty white summer dress
and soft black hair that wafted off her shoulder as she
would tell the kind of rude joke that would make a
whole party bond. "Ri Luo" meant sunset, and that's how I
imagined her, vaulting the sky.

My girlfriend flew home for New Year's, and when she
came back she wanted to talk. She studied my face for a
minute and then said, "I slept with Ri Luo."

My heart stopped beating. We were polyamorous, or at
least I was trying very hard to be. I didn't want to fail
now. I wanted to do and say the right thing. I wanted to
remember what the right thing was. I thought I was
going to pass out. "Her breasts didn't feel like I
remembered," she continued, demonstrating with her
hands.

My body started to shake with rage and humiliation. I got
up and left the room. I was making a scene and I knew it,
but I couldn't remember the right thing to do, or to
feel, or to be. I couldn't remember how to be myself.

I loved her, but it wasn't until long after we broke up
that I started to feel like myself again.

Thea Lim   3:17pm

It flows better this time but I still think that I only
recognize the references because I'm your sister. Maybe

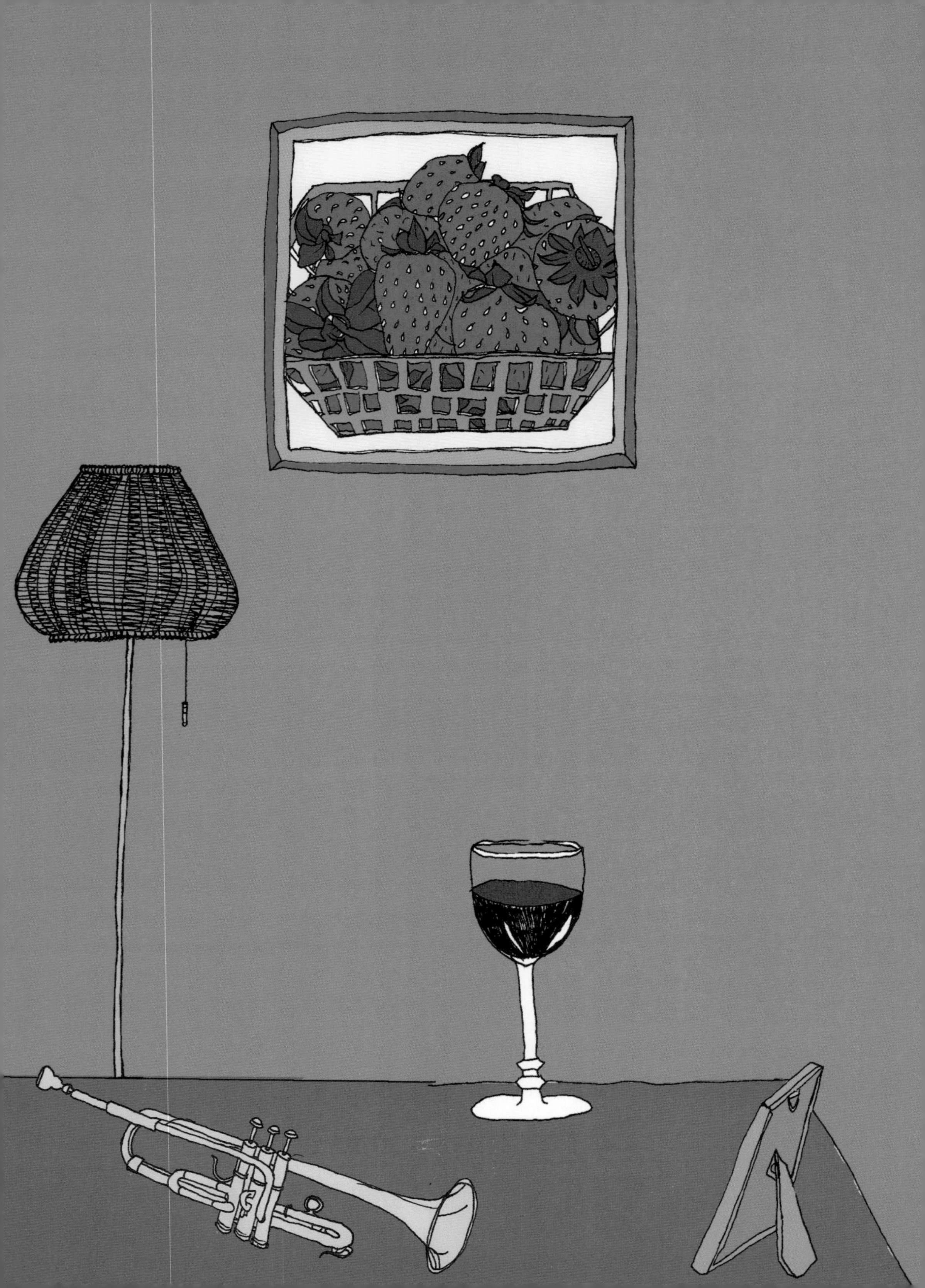

The third woman was my boyfriend's ex. It wasn't that they were still attached. They didn't have an ambiguous relationship. It's just that I was very young. I'd never dated anybody before.

I'd never felt love before him. I loved his sense of humour so much that I made it my own. He made the whole world feel familiar and strange and hilarious and urgent. He was my first kiss, a spectacular kiss that made me run all the way home to calm my heart.

We were in high school and I lived with my parents but he didn't. He was the only guy in class with his own downtown apartment. He was subletting Cheng's apartment until she came back from Manila.

Cheng was his amazing ex-girlfriend, especially to a teenager who'd just learned how to kiss. I never even saw her place, but in my imagination it was a mysterious castle of independence, full of musical instruments and Cheng's own tasteful works of art.

She had left home when she was fifteen and lied successfully about her age to work in the coolest store I knew — The Gap. She was, most exotically, an activist. I didn't even know what that meant, but I decided that she must be passionate and outspoken. Once I asked him, "why would you want to date a kid like me after such a glamorous adult?" "Well honestly," he answered, "sometimes I do miss her."

That was a problem. After we broke up, I still obsessed a bit about the magic lady. When I moved away from home I thought of her, when I got my first job I thought of her, when I got lost in a new city, I thought of her, looking down from a tower of knowledge, probably knowing the way.

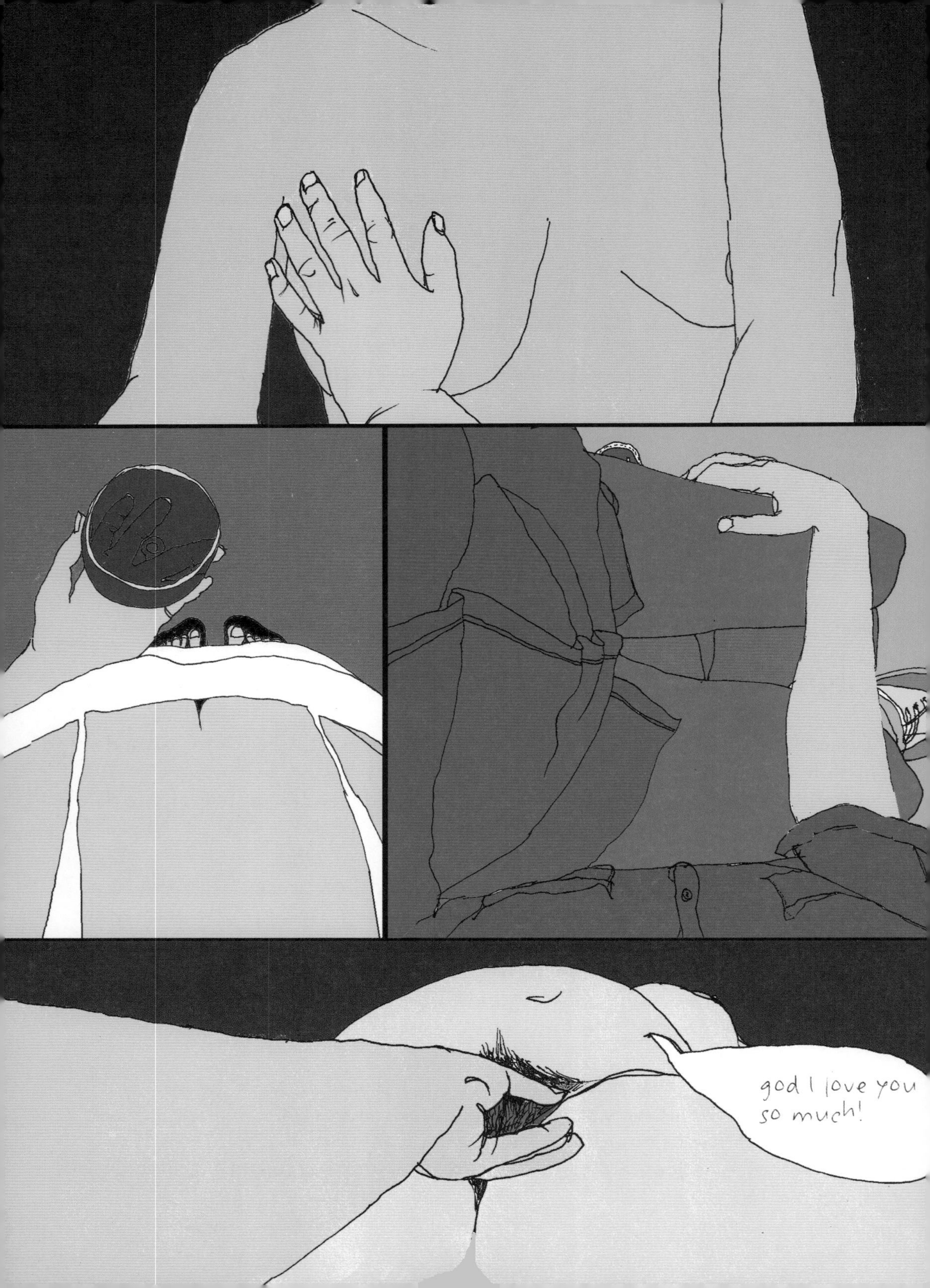
god I love you so much!

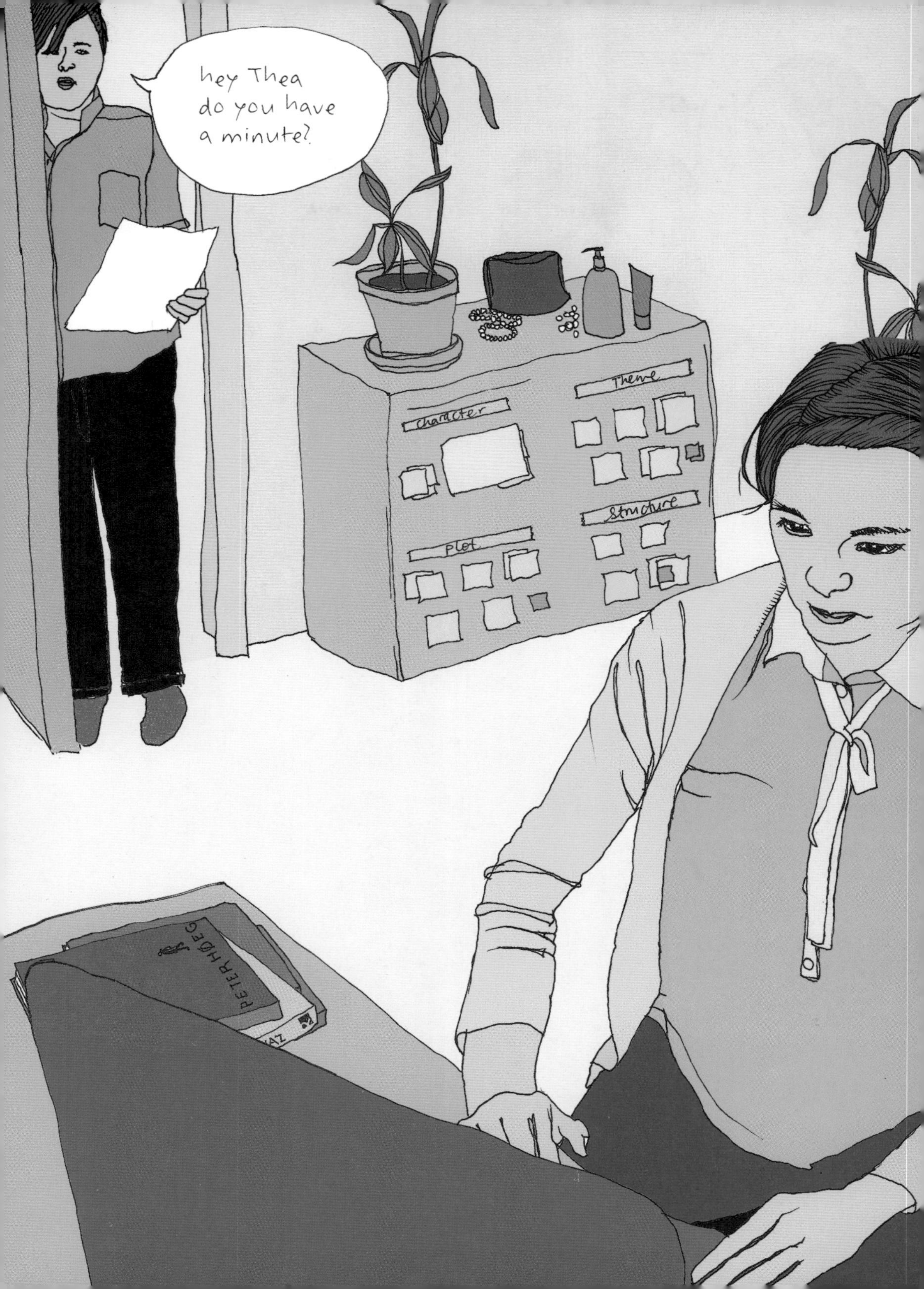
hey Thea
do you have
a minute?
character
Theme
plot
Structure
PETER HØEG

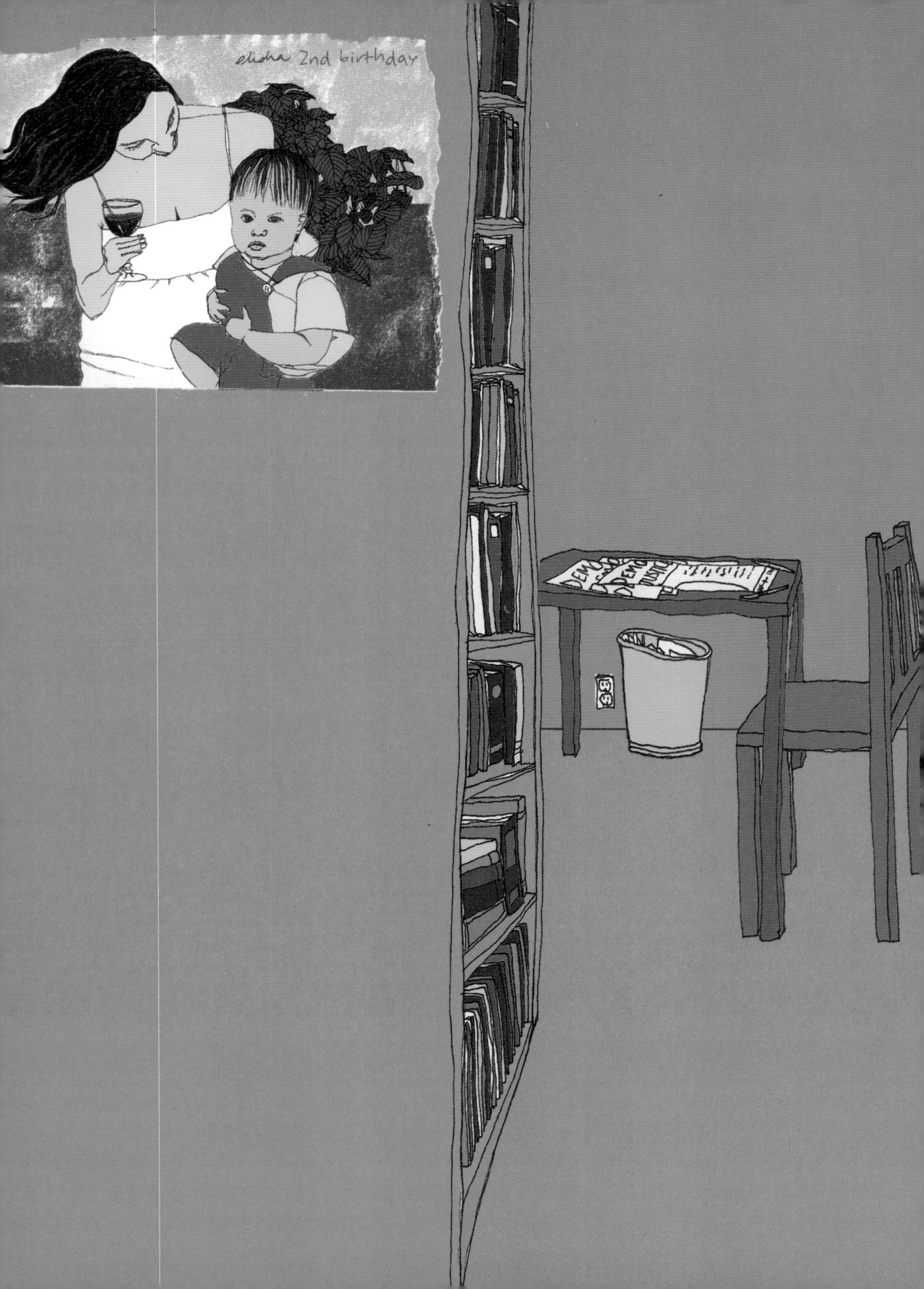
elisha 2nd birthday

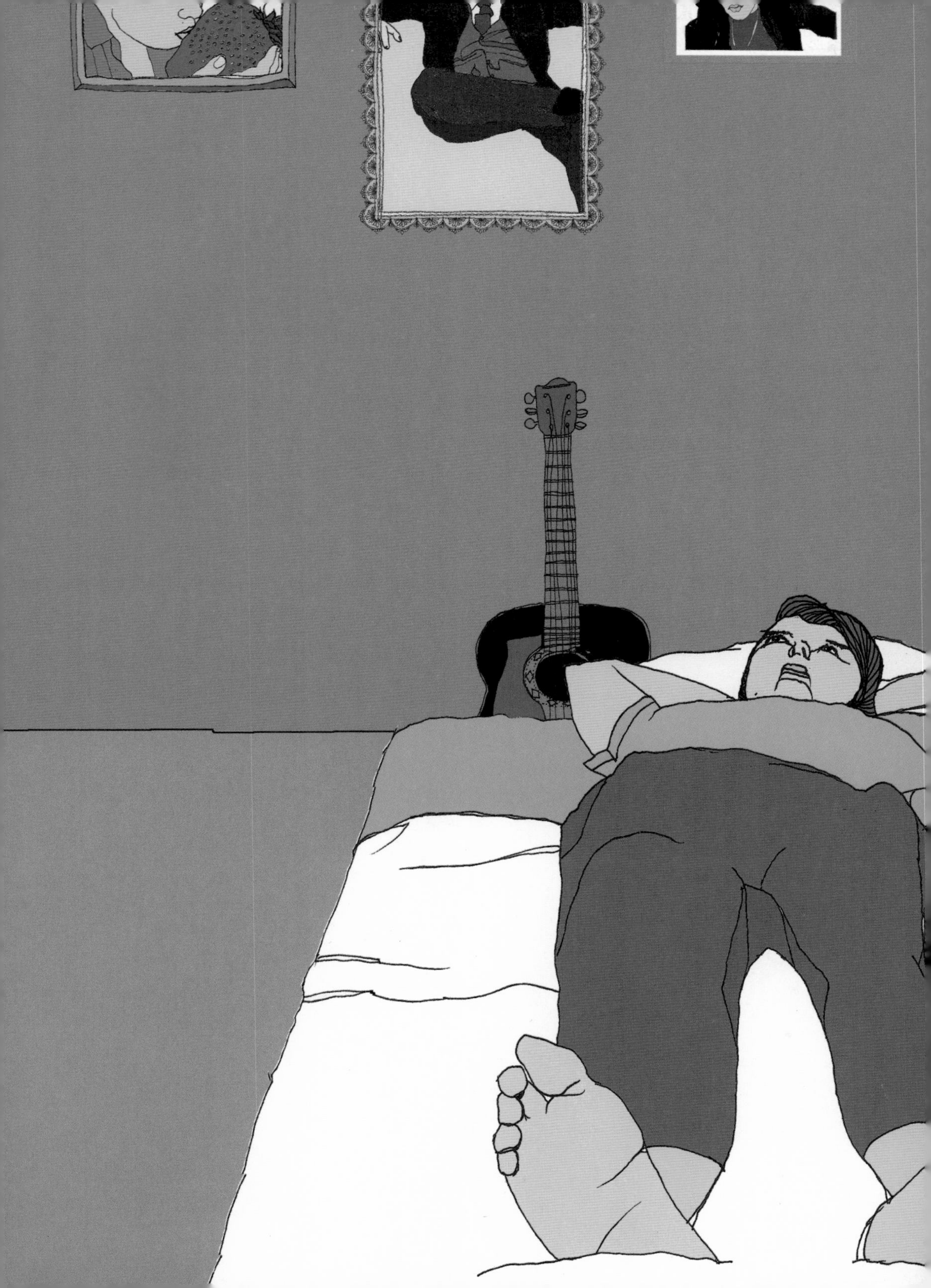

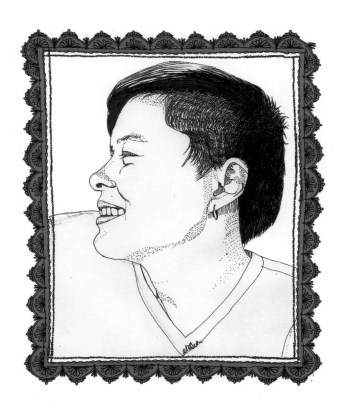

About me, the author

I never went to art school. But when I was 26 a fortune teller told me to quit trying to publish magazines. "Instead," she said, "go back to doing what you loved as a child."
Ba—bang! I have crushes and draw pictures about it. Was she ever right. My illustrated blushes and sighs have been exhibited and published willy nilly — in the legendary FAG gallery, rad magazines like Bitch and Curve, the Gay Genius anthology, the Sister Spit tour and anthology— and they debuted as a claymation at the British Film Institute. I've also had the chance to widen the conversation as a curator in Toronto, a jury member in the States, a festival director in Montreal and an anti—racist activist everywhere.

5 years of queer comi[cs]

Butches, sissies, dandies and convent girls: Eli[sha] Lim adores queers in every town and celebrates them with tributes, interviews and memoirs. This is a collection of five years of tender loving comics about an international gender-bending avant garde.

The emotional honesty of the drawings is matched by Lim's earnestly handwritten text... with a fluency and an immediacy that breaks my heart.
—Alison Bechdel, author of Fun Home and Dykes to Watch Out For

Elisha Lim is one of the world's premier queer visual artists. While reading 100 Crushes, prepare for the personal and the political in a charming combination of images and text.
—Rae Spoon, author of First Spring Grass Fire

$18
Koyama Press

$18.00
ISBN 978-1-92766806-1
51800>

9 781927 668061